ENGAGING
Teens in Their
Own Learning:

8 Keys to Student Success

Dr. Paul J. Vermette

EYE ON EDUCATION
6 DEPOT WAY WEST, SUITE 106
LARCHMONT, NY 10538
(914) 833–0551
(914) 833–0761 fax
www.eyeoneducation.com

Library of Congress Cataloging-in-Publication Data

Vermette, Paul J.
E.N.G.A.G.I.N.G. teens in their own learning : 8 keys to student success /
Paul J. Vermette.
      p. cm.
   ISBN 978-1-59667-094-5
1. Educational innovations—United States. 2. Teenagers—Education—United States. 3. Social participation—United States. I. Title. II. Title:
ENGAGING teens in their own learning.
LB1027.V357 2008
373.18′0973—dc22

                                                    2008026256

10 9 8 7 6 5 4 3

Also Available from EYE ON EDUCATION

Rigor is NOT a Four-Letter Word
Barbara R. Blackburn

Differentiated Assessment
for Middle and High School Classrooms
Deborah Blaz

Handbook on Differentiated Instruction
for Middle and High Schools
Sheryn Spencer Northey

Constructivist Strategies:
Meeting Standards and Engaging Adolescent Minds
Chandra Foote, Paul Vermette, and Catherine Battaglia

Classroom Motivation from A to Z:
How to Engage Your Students in Learning
Barbara R. Blackburn

Classroom Instruction from A to Z:
How to Promote Student Learning
Barbara R. Blackburn

Seven Simple Secrets:
What the BEST Teachers Know and Do!
Annette Breaux and Todd Whitaker

What Great Teachers Do *Differently*:
14 Things That Matter most
Todd Whitaker

Formative Assessment for English Language Arts:
A Guide for Middle and High School Teachers
Amy Benjamin

But I'm Not a Reading Teacher:
Strategies for Literacy Instruction in the Content Areas
Amy Benjamin

Teacher-Made Assessments:
How to Connect Curriculum, Instruction, and Student Learning
Christopher R. Gareis and Leslie W. Grant

Professional Learning Communities:
An Implementation Guide and Toolkit
Kathleen A. Foord and Jean M. Haar

About the Author

Dr. Paul Vermette has been a professional educator since 1971. He has served as a teacher and supervisor of Social Studies in public and parochial schools in New York and New Jersey and has been at Niagara University (NU) in a full-time capacity since 1985. He has authored (or coauthored) three texts on learning from teaching and is the author of over twenty articles on the topics of constructivism, cooperative learning, and concept learning.

Vermette has been a highly visible advocate for teacher professional growth, conducting hundreds workshops and serving as a consultant on both sides of the United States–Canadian border. Vermette has served in various capacities for external agencies and organizations and was President of the Executive Board of New York State ATE in the early 90s. He has also been deeply involved in the activities of the Institute for Learning-Centered Education (Potsdam, NY), The New York State Middle School Association, The New York State Council for Social Studies and the Great Lakes Association for Cooperation in Education (Toronto).

Vermette has been named to Educational Awards several times, the first as a teacher in the Diocese of Buffalo, later as Niagara University Professor of the Year, and for the Neal Appleby Award for New York's Outstanding Teacher Educator in 2007. (He is also Niagara University's candidate for U.S. Professor of the Year in 2008–09.)

Vermette is extraordinarily proud of his former students, NU graduates who have made their marks as superb classroom teachers. This list is lengthy, but includes Jason Blokhuis, Cindy Kline, Susan Hibbard, Toby Marr, Tim Rudan, John Solarski, Dan Johnson, Mary Murray, Edie White, Monica Burgio, Karrie and Jennifer Jones, and Molly Koelle.

The native Western New Yorker and former football coach has been married to Kathleen since 1970, and the couple's one child, Matthew, is another NU grad who is a superb Social Studies teacher, now in the Lockport, NY district.

Among his publications are the following three articles that are relevant here:

Vermette, P.J., & Foote, C.J. (2001). Constructivist philosophy and cooperative learning practice, *American Secondary Education, 30*(1), 26–37.

Vermette, P.J. (1994, March). Four fatal flaws: Avoiding the common mistakes of novice users of cooperative learning. *The High School Journal,* 255–260.

Vermette, P.J., Foote, C.J., Battaglia, C., Mesibov, D., Bird, C., & Harris-Ewing, S. (2000) Understanding constructivism(s): A primer for parents and school board members. *Education, 122*(1), 87–93.

Dedication

I thankfully dedicate this book…

to Matt and Kit
for their unconditional support of my journey

to Cindy, Ted, and Don
who have made my journey very ENGAGING

to Karrie and Jennifer
without whom this book never would have happened…and who will ENGAGE teens for a long time

and to Kate
who helped turn thoughts to prose

Table of Contents

Preface

Here are brief glimpses of three superb secondary school teachers. Their practices offer a taste of what is forthcoming in this text. As you read, look for patterns and identify what you like about their work.

Mr. Ludwig, a seventh grade Biology teacher in rural Oregon, regularly has four-person teams of students (a) choose, (b) investigate, (c) discuss (d) write about and, finally, (e) orally share their learnings from his content area, Life Science. Students can also choose to write reports for their class newsletter, for which extra credit is earned. Each topic is not finished until a visual graphic organizer is created and posted on the wall for a month.

Miss Harris, a twelfth grade Health teacher in a Houston suburb, has students working very hard right up until graduation. They are expected to plan and complete individual projects and to identify connections between the projects and with their local culture. Students keep journals of their daily discussions in class and their readings out of class. Grades are negotiated by the teacher and the students, and rubrics are developed to create a fair (and public) rendering of quality.

Mrs. Queen is a ninth grade English teacher in a "transition" program in Milwaukee. Most of her students are at serious risk of not graduating from high school, and many arrive in ninth grade with a "poor attitude." She emphasizes the importance of setting goals with her students and adapts curriculum to those ends. The students choose literature that speaks to them as people and develop projects that are shared with the class community, frequently working with classmates and always reflecting on their personal behavior.

Three teachers in three grades in three schools in three states in three subjects have much in common: each uses a set of strategies that encourages and directs teenagers into thinking about important school content in ways that help them develop conceptual understanding and make them ready for more thinking.

They use what this book calls the ENGAGING factors—eight strategies that are powerful individually and which combine to present an educational opportunity that speaks to every teenager's individuality; his or her interests, strengths, passions, and concerns; and taps into specific intellectual affective and cognitive strengths, which are developed in a community context that is safe, encouraging, challenging, inviting, and enjoyable.

These teachers have mastered the possible: they have helped each of their teens take ownership of his or her own education and helped each build a community in which everyone is valued. The vision of their successes is the one offered by the ENGAGING process and one that you might find worthy of your deep effort and thoughtful reading.

To get your reading of the book started, here are the eight ENGAGING factors that the three teachers keep in mind as they plan and carry out their daily work:

ENTICE EFFORT and BUILD COMMUNITY: Every opportunity to motivate, encourage and support students is taken.

NEGOTIATE MEANING: Students must develop their own understanding of important ideas; they are never expected to memorize without meaning nor are they to claim understanding without their own examination.

GROUP COLLABORATIVELY: Students work in and out of partnerships; consequently, they must be respectful of everyone else and accept the responsibility of honoring a community of diverse individuals.

ACTIVE LEARNING and AUTHENTIC ASSESSMENT: Learning is seen as the result of thinking and is demonstrated by a performance of understanding. Learning is doing and is always visible and audible; "tests" mean providing evidence of understanding by skilled use of ideas in a new and realistic situation.

GRAPHIC ORGANIZERS: A simplistic but powerful tool, these are used regularly to examine information, record thinking, and to document relationships. Students think visually on a regular basis and keep these as other people keep computer files.

INTELLIGENCE INTERVENTIONS: Diversity is the norm, so differentiated intervention (many based on Multiple Intelligence Theory) has also become the norm. Teachers and students utilize a myriad set of strategies, ideas, and practices to find ones that work for specific individuals.

NOTE MAKING: Unlike most secondary classrooms in which every student is expected to develop a set of "notes" that are identical to the teacher's, note making expects each student to record his or her own ideas as they happen and as questions are being answered. Like a "captain's log," these notes explicate the musings, the analogies, the partial answers, and the insights gathered as students navigate the realities of their investigations.

GRADE WISELY: The least-well-examined phenomena in education, grading practices stand as the real belief system of a teacher. In every case, the teacher should give the benefit of the doubt to the thinker-learner and use the grades as motivators for continued work. The approach to grading a project, an assignment, a homework or an interaction becomes the vehicle by which a teacher defines his or her philosophy and sends messages to teens about their own expectations for success in that class.

These eight factors are easy to understand and implement, yet they grow in complexity, become sophisticated in their deployment, are increasingly powerful in their effectiveness, and hold the distinct promise of helping teachers reach every teen. I hope that you keep reading, thinking, and sharing.

Introduction

I wish to accomplish three things with this book:

1. To offer you a set of teaching suggestions, a coherent strategy, that may be of great value to you as you attempt to engage an increasingly diverse group of teens in thinking, understanding, and learning activities that will enable them to develop the cognitive and affective qualities they will need in their futures.

2. To challenge some of your assumptions and beliefs and create opportunities to resolve the disequilibrium that you are supposed to experience as you consume this book. The book is not to be "read" in a way that suggests that reading is glossing over, skimming, perusing, or glancing through; rather, the book is supposed to be analyzed, compared, dissected, attacked, and questioned. The cases and situations offered are to be examined actively so that each time you finish reading a part of it, you will have some new ideas and insights for your own practice.

3. To have you feel optimistic about the prospects of having *every* teenager profit from his or her schooling and learn to appreciate the ENGAGING factors as they work to help teens to think deeply about important school content. In truth, we have no models for reaching every teen—no culture has ever done it (few have even tried), but contemporary schools have set high expectations for this goal and the means may be at our fingertips.

The Structure of the Book

Chapter 1 presents the example of Mrs. Reallygood, a high school science teacher who attempts to use all eight aspects of the ENGAGING approach. It introduces these eight factors and places them in a valuable context.

Chapter 2 offers some lengthy case studies of social studies teachers and builds the case for each of the eight aspects of ENGAGING. Its title, *Elaborations, Differentiations, and Inte-*

E	entice effort
N	negotiate meaning
G	group collaboratively
A	active learning
G	graphic organizers
I	intelligence interventions
N	note making
G	grade wisely

grations spells out the rationale for this set of factors. It closes with another example, this one set in the Middle School.

Chapters 1 and 2 help you develop sound answers to these *essential questions:* "How does one teach so that every teen can develop meaningful understanding?" (Thanks to Wiggins & McTighe, 2005); and "How do the eight ENGAGING factors actually work in a teacher's practice?"

Some may see Chapter 3 as unnecessary because it focuses on scholarly support for the ENGAGING approach, which some teachers may dismiss. Yet I maintain that this support is an essential part of my argument and theory. Essentially, practice has led to theory and back to practice and this chapter aligns the ENGAGING approach with a supportive scholarly base. I have provided annotations for six great books, eight powerful research articles and ten fascinating articles that all secondary teachers should be familiar with. Although some of us who teach in grades 5 to 12 still don't accept the challenge to grow in terms of available scholarship, the work presented here speaks volumes to practitioners wishing to change their routines. The *essential question* here is: "Why should I believe that these ENGAGING factors work?"

Chapter 4 offers some ideas about using the ENGAGING process; appropriately, it starts with the first-day-of-school efforts of three first-year math teachers in a suburban setting. Their cases contrast markedly, enabling you to critique and offer suggestions to them—and to yourself.

You are also provided with the cases of three outstanding secondary teachers who have been very successful for a long time: Dave Watkins is a history teacher in metropolitan Toronto; Beth Konkoski-Bates is an English teacher in suburban Virginia; and Maureen Russell is a science teacher in rural New York State. In each case, engagement was the teacher's highest priority and there is much to ponder in their stories.

There is also a section on cooperative learning. As a system, nothing has been more effective to improve test scores, increase conceptual understanding, create a sense of community, or develop interpersonal skills than cooperative learning. Ideas about its implementation are offered here because incorporating ENGAGING into cooperative learning may hold the biggest promise of success possible.

Chapter 4 also carefully differentiates between two types of *practice*. Actually, these are paradigmatic differences essential to designing powerful in-class activities and out-of-class assignments and projects. Constructivist alternatives, such as those ENGAGING offers, need to be supported by the right kind of "practice," "study," and "task."

Finally, two contemporary concepts are examined in the hypothetical case of the Reallygoods (Chris and Lee). *Collaboration* between teachers and between students and *differentiation* (the fostering of different avenues to student understanding of important content) are two natural pathways followed by those who use the ENGAGING factors. Their scenario lets us see it in action, giving us an example to explore and modify.

Finally, the chapter closes with an adaptation of the Six Facets of Understanding offered by Wiggins and McTighe (2005). A self-assessment about the ENGAGING process follows this design and enables the reader to develop a clear sense of accomplishment. In the spirit of our contemporary accountability issues, I have called this piece the *Final Examination*, and it is "high stake" because it predicts how well you will examine your own practice.

The *essential questions* addressed here are these: "How do I get started?" and "What else should I be thinking about as I seek to get better?"

1

One Class in the Life...ENGAGING Mrs. Reallygood's Students

Essential Question

How does one teach so that every teen is valued and can develop meaningful understanding?

Mrs. Reallygood

Jose, 15 years old, is a tenth grader at Roosevelt High School in Big City, USA. He is sitting in his third period science class with twenty-five others adolescents. He is fortunate because his teacher, Mrs. Reallygood, is a first-class teacher. She wants her students and their classes to be thoughtful, meaningful, and joyful, and she understands that each learner is a unique individual. She is a "master teacher" and her charges enjoy the experience of her class, realize that they are learning a lot, and are going to pass the dreaded state assessments in June. They know they must work together so that each can succeed. Ramona, who was classified

E	entice effort
N	negotiate meaning
G	group collaboratively
A	active learning
G	graphic organizers
I	intelligence interventions
N	note making
G	grade wisely

as a "slow learner" when she went to private school, is doing well and also likes this class. She used to dislike Jose immensely because he always acted tough and "picked on" her and her friends, Jill and Mandy, but that doesn't happen any more, either in class or out.

Class started at 10:00. An observer, using a modified shadow technique, observed the class and focused on Ramona and Jose. Brief interviews were conducted to gather confirming statements. Here are the observer's notes. Please read the passage to interpret the quality of the teaching. (Consider jotting down your own comments on a piece of paper.)

10:03 Both Jose and Ramona are busy making a list of things they know about the respiratory system with their assigned teammates. Each offers a couple of ideas that make it onto the team list and each is keeping a personal list on butcher block paper that will be displayed later. Over the teacher's desk is a sign that reads "How my lungs work…and why I care," which is the theme of the unit and their assignment.

10:07 Jose was interested and attended thoughtfully as two students, including Ramona, told stories of how loved ones had gotten lung cancer and died at a young age. He, himself, has a touch of asthma, although he hasn't shared that information widely, and he thinks about how his own alveoli are similar to the ones of the people in the stories.

10:09 Reallygood knows about Jose's health and gives him a quick look when a long-distance runner, Tim, tells about the effects of his training. Jose raises his hand and discloses to class about the ways that he has worked on his lungs. While sharing the story, Reallygood walks over behind him, stands nodding her head and smiling at him gently the whole time. She does speak once, offering a technical comment about oxygenated blood as Jose stops, listens carefully, and then continues.

10:23 The students are reading a short passage from a magazine about a teen with a lung problem who lives in a heavily polluted city. Each student has been asked to fill out a sheet called a Venn diagram, which will be compared to those generated by classmates in a few minutes. Ramona, who has reading difficulties, is quietly chatting with Jill who helps her with the passage and completion of the form.

10:32 As they are working together, Reallygood asks each student to personally draft a single sentence about what they thought the reading meant. (All do the task quickly.) Pairs of students informally share their sentences. Ramona tells Mandy about the dangers of smoking and Jose explains to Felix about how lungs operate differently when they are damaged.

10:40 As she makes her way around the room, Reallygood stops by Jose's desk and tells him that his sentence would make a great opening for his essay. Caught off guard, Jose is pleased and makes a mental note of her comment. Then Reallygood asks him to help Mandy with her wording; he grunts an "OK" and slides his desk over to help her. Ramona is asking Jill about several word meanings and Reallygood chooses to leave them alone. She drifts from desk to desk, reading over the students' shoulders.

10:54 The students are now working individually on their writing. Reallygood walks by Jose's desk and adjusts his scrap notes so that he can see them; touching them has caused him to reexamine them. The process has also made the sheet called "rubric" become visible again. "Pretty good so far," is all she says.

11:08 Reallygood interrupts the entire class by asking for one minute of their time. She wants them all to state one thing that they have thought deeply about during class that day. "Tell your neighbor," she requests. When the noise dims, she calls on five students to tell their ideas to the whole class—they represent the variety of ideas present around the room. Every student has his or her idea represented and then they are thanked and told to get back to work.

11:21 Reallygood calls on Jerome, a large and hulking young man. He is asked to tell why he thinks they are writing this narrative. Seemingly surprised, he slowly says, "Well, we gotta know about…well, science and lungs and stuff…to help…you know…stay healthy." Reallygood smiles and says to all, "You have thirty seconds to come up with three reasons. Please chat with those around you." One minute later, she calls on Jerome again and then three others (including Ramona), each of whom has a good reason. As she tells the class to finish up and get ready to go to the next class, she writes the four reasons on the board.

11:24 As the students leave the room, Reallygood stands by the door and nods and smiles at each student. Holding a stack of rubrics in her left hand, Reallygood uses her right hand to wave or give a "thumbs up" sign. (She shakes hands with Jerome and gives a sloppy "high five" to Mandy.) She does remind them all that they should plan to work hard on their writing and finish it over the next few days.

Reflection Time

What did you think of this class? What did you think about the assignment, the material being considered, and the role the teacher chose to play? What did you think of the teacher's use of time? How did Reallygood treat the students? How were students motivated to think deeply and carefully? How did the students seem to enjoy the experience? What was expected of them? What else could have been done to make the class more productive? In short: How good was this class?

As you analyze and evaluate her work, I ask you to ponder the following eight questions, which directly align with the eight factors involved in the ENGAGING process that I promote and articulate as the central theme of this book. Simply put, if we really *care* about teenagers and if their lives do "matter," the eight factors can be very powerful instructional tools. In some ways they have been foreshadowed in this exercise, but I ask that you articulate an answer for each of the following questions and ask you to reread segments of the description to clarify your own thinking.

1. How did the teacher get the students to do the meaningful thinking that was expected of them and how did she nurture positive relationships with each student?

2. How did the teacher get Ramona and Jose to think deeply about the essential content and concepts so that the ideas made personal sense?

3. How did the teacher develop a sense of belonging and the feeling of community so that everyone could interact safely and productively?

4. How did the teacher create and utilize opportunities for feedback for the efforts and accomplishments of every student?

5. How did the teacher use strategies and activities that helped learners organize, scaffold, and record their developing ideas?

6. How did the teacher use planned activities and spontaneous interactions to promote the learning efforts of Ramona and Jose?

7. How did the teacher assist students to document their own understandings of major ideas and organize them so they could be used and examined?

8. How did the teacher use "grades and marks" to promote a sense of justice and to avoid decreasing student effort?

Take a moment to reflect on your responses to these eight questions and to compare them with your original thinking as requested by the set of questions at the beginning of this section.

Eight *ENGAGING* Factors Described

The eight factors of the ENGAGING process are reintroduced in the narrative below. It is my contention that we are in the midst of a paradigm shift, moving to one that is student-thinking centered and away from the teacher-information-presenting one of traditional classrooms. Research in psychology and neurology supports this shift, and our history of failure with so many adolescents demands it. As you read over these eight factors, think again of Reallygood's practices, your response to the eight questions above, and your interpretation of what her classroom looks like. Please keep your *vision* of her efforts in mind as you consider the key factors in the ENGAGING process.

E entice effort and encourage continuously, building positive relationships at every opportunity

N negotiate meaningful understanding of essential content by each individual

G group collaboratively, building and sustaining a community of thinkers and learners

A active learning strategies and assessments allow for frequent feedback and reinforcement

G graphic organizers provide structural prompts to help thinkers manage information and ideas

I interventions, both carefully planned activities and spontaneous interactions with individuals, build relationships, personal responsibility, and cognitive understandings

N note making, a process whereby a student records his or her own thinking and meaning, is far more powerful than the traditional note taking, which focused on simply transcribing information

G grade (mark) students and their work judiciously, for it can be a powerful motivator or a great source of discouragement

These eight factors all overlap, reinforce each other, and carry some essential themes that stand directly as advice to secondary teachers:

♦ Care about the individual and know him or her as unique and valuable;

♦ Expect students to think deeply by solving complex intellectual problems, relating to ideas personally, or creating something new;

♦ Embed social, emotional, and cognitive skill development in meaningful works of conceptualization;

- Make schoolwork an enjoyable, safe, and self-revealing process;

- Use activities that are structured to entice teens to create and share thought and which encourage students to willfully take ownership of their own education; and

- Do everything possible to build a sense of community within your classroom.

As you will learn later in the chapter, many theorists support the focus that has been placed on these eight factors. Glasser (1986), for example, sees motivation tied to fun, freedom, a sense of belonging, and power—all of which are represented here. Bruner (1996) acknowledges the central focus on concept development. Gardner (1983) recognizes unique sets of intelligences and asks that teachers adjust accordingly. Ladson-Billings' (1994) culturally relevant teaching (CRT) places the individual's personal and cultural experiences at the center of every lesson. Vygotsky (1962) recognizes the power of conversation as an essential learning tool and sees much of the process as interactive in nature. Piaget's (1963) theories certainly support the need for an individual's continuous analysis of ideas, and Dewey's (1916) call for "investigations" laid the theoretical groundwork for the entire process.

So, one may ask, how did Reallygood measure up? The answer to that question varies with each of you; you are all unique, you have had different prior experiences, you have responded differently to the passage and my narrative, and you are at different places in your professional journeys. As I briefly articulate my judgments of her use of the ENGAGING process, I acknowledge that there may well be great differences among my readers, and I hope that these interpretations will be the source of further dialogue. Of course, I am confident about the wisdom of my judgments and hope you find them valuable as well.

Factor 1: Relationships and Student Effort

It is clear that Reallygood has built very positive relationships with her students. By urging Jose to share his "asthma" story, she shows confidence in him and an abiding support for his personality and his pride. She did not force him to disclose but recognized that he wanted to share and trust his classmates and she supported his inclination. She knew that it was good for Jose to be an integral part of the rationale for the lesson *and* saw clearly that classmates would respect him for sharing. She also created the safe environment necessary for this decision to happen. Later in the learning session, she sees quality in his writing and then correctly praises that achievement (Good & Brophy, 2008).

There are several other indicators that suggest Reallygood's relationships are generally functional. She expects students to offer their ideas publicly and always receives those ideas in a positive light. She challenges their perceptions and their concepts, and clearly thinks that they are capable, insightful, and bright young people: she understands that their experiences are real and personal and that any new ideas must connect to the ones they already have (Ladson-Billings, 1994; Bransford, Brown, & Cocking, 2000).

Finally, her strategies to support Ramona are fascinating. Her pairing of Ramona with Mandy is respectful and productive, and it results in Ramona trying hard to do the assigned task. She allows Ramona to get public encouragement when her "reason for the lesson" is one of the five chosen for public display. Finally, her "goofy or sloppy" high five with Ramona at the end of class suggests that they could share a laugh with each other. Breaking bread and laughing together are two ways that people develop "connection," and Reallygood uses the latter approach very well in this scenario.

Note that there is no evidence that this teacher relies on the formal authority of her position to command respect and compliance. The classroom "feels" like a safe place where students come to think, share, and be respected for their learning efforts. The various noisy parts are indicative of this intention. Developing this system demands that the teacher have a clear vision of how class should operate, how people should be treated, and how to get there: it was Reallygood's number one priority at the beginning of the school year and now runs itself.

Every student loves a class like this and does not want to do anything to "lose it." Some still make mistakes and violate the teacher's expectations, but they are the exceptions and are treated that way.

Factor 2: Student-Centered Understanding

Perhaps the most essential point about secondary teaching is that to get the meaningful, deep, and useful conceptual understanding that is demanded by the various standards in use, the students individually must do rigorous, personal, and continuous thinking. Teaching is not the presentation of information by the teacher, but the engagement of the learner with the information.

Teaching is *not* telling; teaching is "sparking thinking."

To me, useful thinking is *not* attempts at remembering but attempts at using information. Bloom's levels of synthesis and analysis force integration of content and one must do it willfully. While rewards may induce people to try to think deeply, only the learner herself can do the thinking process necessary for learning to take place. (Piaget's process of assimilation and accommodation applies here, as does Bruner's concept attainment process.)

Secondary teachers have a long history of being fascinated by the details of their disciplines and seem anxious to share as much minutiae as possible with teens. However, all of that information is external, whereas student understanding is internal and is best thought of as the "knowledge" the student has available.

Again—information is external, knowledge is internal. Teaching is about getting kids to construct their own meanings and recognize that they have done so.

From this perspective, "motivating teens to think deeply" is approximately 99% of our teaching job. Reallygood has used several strategies to increase the likelihood that this happens in her class:

♦ Class opens with the students listing their own experiences and understandings and all participate. Werner (2005) says that teachers "must loosen the soil before the seed can start to take"—his analogy is perfect and applies here. Typically, lecture comes first and is followed by a practice session, but in this case, any lecture will come after the students are ready and will connect with many of the ideas they have already generated (Flynn, Mesibov, Vermette and Smith, 2004).

♦ Each student is expected to do "think work" often; e.g., interpret a reading passage, write a summary sentence, verbally share an experience, and eventually produce the authentic task of the passage. All of this, by the way, is "upper-level Bloom."

♦ Importantly, Reallygood is not wasting student time by littering this session with detailed information that is not needed here. (It can be introduced later, when and if the students are ready for it.) Wiggins and McTighe (2005), Covey (1999), and Tomlinson and McTighe (2006) all strongly suggest that teachers start "with the end in mind," that is, focus on what is "essential" and get every student working to that end. Reallygood has mastered that difficult perspective and her students will pass the standardized tests they face *because*, not in spite of, this trait—they will think deeply about the key ideas and concepts and not be overwhelmed by "trivia."

Factor 3: Group for Collaborative Community

Reallygood has the students working in various structures: they think alone, in volunteer pairs, with others in the room, and as a large group. Her groupings develop student interactions and respect across all parties and support Glasser's "sense of belonging." (Flexible grouping is also a staple of Tomlinson's "differentiation.")

She nurtures the students' work with each other to increase the number of ideas and feedback opportunities *and* to destroy the negative effects of competition (Kohn, 2006) or indifference (Johnson & Johnson, 1999). Everyone is a "player" in her system.

In this class, Reallygood's use of Jerome's response to call for "think-pair-share" forces a sense of community, as does her frequent call for partner sharing.

We don't see it in this session, but the students are in formal four-person teams that regularly meet and work on projects and support each other. Composition of these teams change over time so that eventually, every student works face-to-face with every other one (Vermette, 1998).

Factor 4: Feedback for Student Thought

If you've read the preceding three factors, you will readily recognize that the class is actively engaged at almost all times. Because of this approach, students get feedback from other students on a regular basis. Emotional support for effort coming from *other teens* may be the biggest motivational factor available for a secondary student. To be respected by peers for thinking in school is awesome.

Some teachers may say that they could not envision this ever happening, yet notice that the sense of community exists and the fact that every student does have something of value to share makes this process a natural one, not artificial. There is no "faked praise" here; students think, then share, and then react respectfully.

Cognitive support or feedback on the quality of the thinking can also come from students. But notice that Reallygood "works the room" (Konkoski-Bates & Vermette, 2004) beautifully: She sees and comments on Jose's sentence (and everyone else's), she has listed proper vocabulary so students will begin using it aloud ("alveoli"), and her (passive) nonintervention at various times is quiet support for accuracy.

In traditional classes, mistakes and misconceptions are not usually caught until the test comes and the damage is done. Moreover, these mistakes and misconceptions are rarely rectified.

Under the ENGAGING process, the teacher concentrates on what each student "is thinking about important content" and mistakes are clearly noticeable and can be dealt with in a strategic manner.

Factor 5: Use of Graphic Organizers

Often students get rudimentary ideas but "jumble them all up," confusing connections and creating garbled understandings. This can be disheartening and disabling, causing students to feel alienated or incompetent, especially when literacy processes are involved. In short, many students do not read well. The use of the Venn diagram enables Reallygood's students to identify important information and structure it systematically. They are still doing the learning-work but it is not a haphazard or messy process.

Interestingly, this class use of rubrics may seem like a feedback thing (and it is), but it is also an organizer of sorts. A rubric suggests a systematic way of looking for "quality" and enables the students to use external references for judging and organizing their work.

We don't see other examples of organizers at work in this session, but Reallygood regularly uses the following in addition to the Venn diagram:

♦ The T-Bar to induce a compare and contrast dichotomy type of student analysis;

♦ The Crystal Ball (Basko & Konkoski-Bates, 2005) to introduce new vocabulary and foreshadow a new unit;

♦ The fishbone to help students "see" (literally) the complexity of a topic;

♦ The concept map to help them "see" connections between ideas;

♦ The KWL (Know-Want-Learn) model (Ogle, 1986) where students define what needs to be learned and then document it happening.

(*Note:* Some readers may have seen opportunities for the use of these or other graphic organizer strategies in Reallygood's lesson. Every piece of teaching can be improved or tweaked.)

Factor 6: Interventions to Spark Thinking-Learning

Flynn et al. (2004) speak of planned interventions and spontaneous interventions. The former consist of all the planned activities that Reallygood's used in the class: the opening listing, the public sharing, the reading passage, the key sentence writing, the distribution of the rubric, the writing time, and the partner work. Moreover, even though it may have appeared to be a casual thing, her stopping class to debate the rationale for the assignment was planned: she waited until they had invested some time and effort and then asked them what they thought. She planned to have them work first, and then try to recognize the value of their labor, which they did.

Every time the students are working, Reallygood is "teaching by intervention" (Mesibov, 2003). If she leaves them alone, she makes a decision; if she comments or questions, she makes a decision. Phil Jackson (1994) says that teachers make "1000 important decisions each day." Looking at Reallygood in this class suggests that his total may be an underestimate!

Because she realizes that their thinking *causes* their understanding, she proceeds thoughtfully when she intervenes. Her spontaneous interventions include encouraging Jose, talking about oxygenated blood, urging Jose to help Mandy, touching Jose's notes, calling on Jerome, and her farewell gestures. These are all intended to help individuals continue their work, be proud of their ideas, reexamine a concept, and build community.

Factor 7: Making Notes Is a Thoughtful Process

We all remember the days of college classes: professors talking and talking and students frantically writing everything that they think they hear into notebooks (or, in some cases, students sitting passively waiting for the next class). Students were expected to sit quietly, listen intently, write notes, and go home to "study" their notes. Remembering the professor's words (and ideas) was the goal and reissuing those ideas on a test was a mark of excellence. Notes were a combination of a system of shorthand and a memory enhancer.

Research on note taking has a long history and this body of evidence suggests that the best notes are the ones that students make themselves, which are done with their own words and own thoughts and are tied to a system that works for the individual (Kierwa, 1987). From that perspective, notes are a form of thought recording in which the students' thinking is publicly documented and available for analysis. My term for this is "note making," which is far different from traditional note taking.

In note making, the individual student has to think, solve a problem, create a meaning, make a decision, search her own memories and experiences, and record it. When secondary teachers expect students to do this process, they are calling for customized understandings and show respect for individual's experiences and their attempts at making meaning. Actually, they are a visible (and perhaps audible) manifestation of internal thought.

Reallygood does this well, expecting her students to physically record ideas at many points in the session. Note that her students make a list of their background knowledge at the outset, they complete their Venn diagrams, they write their own sentence, and they work on their narratives. Each requires an investment of note making or writing time and effort that allows ideas to be reexamined later.

Without criticizing her work, I note that she could have incorporated multiple intelligences here without much trouble. Encoding with a drawing or a chart may have been beneficial to some students; it is still a visible record-keeping process. (She may well ask students to "draw or write" on certain occasions.) Science demonstrations allow physical engagement with materials and allow students to kinesthetically encode ideas. Regardless, the contemporary emphasis on literacy suggests that using written note-making processes may prove most beneficial to most students most of the time.

It is interesting that this teacher frequently uses "outslips" to get students to reflect on their accomplishments that day. Although these can be thought of as forms of assessment data gathering, they are also useful as record-keeping experiences for students.

Imagine Jose completing these five statements as he left Reallygood's room that day:

1. One thing that I learned today is that…

2. It helped me a lot when my classmate…

3. I still wonder about…

4. One new (science) word that I now feel comfortable using is _____, which means…

5. I hope that I never forget that …

Although there are "millions" of these outslip items possible, here are seven more that you might find intriguing at this point in time:

1. One thing from today that will be on the test is …

2. Today, my teacher really emphasized…

3. The stuff we thought about is important because…

4. If I could, I'd like to read more about…

5. Other teens should know that …

6. What wasted my time today was…

7. By having us work with each other…

In each of these completions, the student response is valuable because it is personalized meaning, connected to the curriculum, indicative of understanding, and reflective of the experience the student had that day. When teachers think adolescents matter, they take this kind of data very seriously and use it to adjust their future interactions and interventions.

Factor 8: Grade Carefully and Wisely

In many places, secondary schooling has become "all about grades." The only reinforcers in many teachers' bag of tricks are "points." They give zeroes for missed work, take "points off" for spelling, give bonus points for extra work, and so on. Grading has always been a very idiosyncratic process and only recently has the grading process begun to appear as a topic in teacher's workshops, professional literature (O'Connor, 2002), and their list of concerns.

Make no mistake, grades *are* important. They are a symbol of achievement and have localized meaning to parents, employers, the military, coaches, and even to teens themselves. The advice here is to grade judiciously, meaning to avoid using them as punishers (the "hammer") or to identify weak students to justify stratification systems. The best use of grades is to motivate students to achieve understanding of important ideas, to create a sense of fairness and justice, and to clarify expectations.

Reallygood grades students daily, using a five-point scale (Vermette, 1998). The daily grades earned over a period of time are collected and used as an indicator of (a) an individual's contribution to others, (b) the students' conceptual knowledge developed internally (see note making above) during class time, and (c) experiences that show potential as a responsible citizen and worker. These three goals—collaborating and exchanging ideas, making meaning, and working responsibly as a citizen and worker—are explicit goals for her course (and, e.g., in New York, linked directly to the state standards).

Even though this single grade is subsequently weighted with other assessment measures for a course grade, the process indicates that each class does matter and that each student also matters.

This purposefulness is often missing in secondary classes; many students see little connection between a specific class (or an assignment) and the real world, including their own lives. Dewey once said that school *is life*, not just preparation for life and Reallygood acts as if he was correct.

I think that she does grade wisely. Class grades are accepted by students as absolutely "fair." Everyone is considered important, everyone can contribute (there are no perceived "favorites"), everyone has to work, and she collects their made-notes and outslips often, so their work is recognized.

Her use of rubrics makes expectations for the assignment explicit. Moreover, by helping students do some of their work right in class, students think of her as trying hard to get them to succeed.

At no time does Reallygood bargain, or negotiate, or threaten, using grades as a lever. An atmosphere of threat, not uncommon in middle and high schools, is actually a demotivator—if a youth has not internalized the value of a good grade, being threatened with a bad one simply reinforces alienation and justifies poor behavior and the type of attitude that poisons many classrooms. Without any hope or sense of success (Glasser's classic meaning for the term *power*) students clearly feel as if they don't matter and that they shouldn't even try.

> Grading processes should indicate what has been gained,
> *not* what has been lost.

Reallygood has evidence of all kinds that Ramona and Jose have "thought well" on essential questions on this day. Their positive grades, hopefully seen as a reward, have been *earned* and genuinely reflect a greater level of cognitive achievement than they had before class began. And everybody in class knows it; there is justice.

For many students, little successes are *huge*. Little defeats are also huge. Grading is anything but neutral in this atmosphere.

In Closing

From my perspective, we have seen a pretty good piece of teaching in Reallygood's class. She has engaged every student and delivered on her plan to have them think often and deeply about important content. They are aware of their growth and are generally proud of it. She has noted "where they are" cognitively and can effectively reflect on what to do next. Each student feels respected and valued, by their teacher and, most importantly, by the student's peers. School makes sense in their lives, now and for the future. Science is seen as very fundamental to understanding health-related ideas, which are, of course, important. School matters—and so does every teen in the room.

2

Enhancing ENGAGING: Elaborations/ Integrations/ Differentiations

Essential Question

How do the eight ENGAGING factors actually work in a teacher's practice?

This chapter sets out to accomplish three things:

1. In the first section, I want you to think deeply about the practice of several high school social studies teachers who are experimenting with several innovations simultaneously: backward planning (Wiggins & McTighe, 2005), the Two-Step (Flynn et al., 2004), and some of the eight ENGAGING factors, including active learning, the use of graphic organizers, and note making. By comparing

E	entice effort
N	negotiate meaning
G	group collaboratively
A	active learning
G	graphic organizers
I	intelligence interventions
N	note making
G	grade wisely

and contrasting these three men's efforts to change, you will get a deeper understanding of the importance of instructional differences and begin to track their implications. You will also start to see how ENGAGING can help them make good decisions and be more effective in reaching adolescents.

2. In the second section, I offer a lengthy narrative, taking you inside each of the eight factors. Hopefully, you will see the logic of every factor and grasp the significance of the examples offered for each one. You may easily adapt the examples to your own practice.

3. Finally, in the third section, I offer the case of Mr. Reallygood (a relative of Mrs. Reallygood, the science teacher you met in Chapter 1) and another social studies teacher (although at the Middle School). As you read this Reallygood scenario, you will see how the initial cases and the narrative have combined to spark your interpretation of ENGAGING, build your understanding of it in practice, and prepare you to read Chapter 3, which offers a mountain of supporting evidence for its power.

Introducing Mr. Bee and Mr. Cee (and Mr. Dee): ENGAGING Pearl Harbor

Pearl Harbor Unit

Here are twenty possible student activities that could be used be used in a high school unit on Pearl Harbor. Please look the items over and then divide them into three groups: one group marked *E* for use *early* in the unit, one marked *L* for *late* in the unit, and one marked *M* for *middle* of the unit.

_____ a. Students write six of their own questions about Pearl Harbor

_____ b. Students sketch four visuals of the bombing while looking at textbook photo spread

_____ c. Students watch an eight-minute [documentary] film loop of the attack

_____ d. Students choose ten questions from a list of twenty teacher-provided ones and begin with researching them in class, using a variety of technological and print resources

_____ e. Students hear tapes of three different men reading Roosevelt's "Infamy" speech

_____ f. Students individually find Hawaii on globe and map and identify Pearl Harbor

_____ g. Students make a personal list of things they already know about attack and share

_____ h. Students write a 100-word reflection on their ideas about the attack

_____ i. Students read a four-paragraph description from text-book

_____ j. Students read six pages from a novel about the attack

_____ k. Students share their knowledge and opinions with three other students

_____ l. Students make a T-bar of reasons for Congress to say "yes or no" to war

_____ m. Students create their own five-page book called "Pearl Harbor: My View"

_____ n. Students listen while teacher gives a five-minute background narrative about the attack

_____ o. Students do a "word search" puzzle for eight key terms

_____ p. Students work in class on their projects/assignments

_____ q. Students take an examination (twenty-five multiple-choice and one essay)

_____ r. Students identify words that conceptually relate to the various letters in the phrase SURPRISE ATTACK

_____ s. Students watch twelve minutes from the movie "Tora! Tora! Tora!"

_____ t. Students write the answers to five "Main Idea" questions on page 999 in text

As an aside: Remember that this very task (creating the flow and sequence of the students learning activities plus group sharing and analysis) was the focus of a professional development experience that led to the experimentations and rethinking done by the three teachers whose implementation you will examine in a few moments. But first…a reaction to _your_ sequencing is needed.

Author Comments

There are several noteworthy notions about the groupings into early (E), middle (M), and late (L) that you did in the above activity. First, you probably have built groups of items, rather than left singletons in any one category. That categorization scheme is consistent with Flynn et al.'s notion of the Two-Step: teachers need to plan and conduct Exploratory activities (plural) that begin the process of investigation, motivate across diversities, and call up the necessary prior experiences. These were your E category. Note that Hunter's (1982) famous "anticipatory set" was usually interpreted as a single "hook" that was done quickly in the beginning and which was supposed to move every teen equally. It is more likely that a series of activities would engage more students more deeply than would a single, undifferentiated, and brief event.

Your L category represents Flynn et al.'s Discovery phase in which students actually do the work required for them to deeply process ideas, put a personal touch on them and demonstrate their new understanding. The Discovery involves the graded work. Item "m", "making their own five-page book," is the most frequently selected final activity in most people's L category; it appears to be the most commonly chosen final project for the unit, but does *not* stand as the only graded work in the unit.

The items you have marked as M (middle) could fit into either of Flynn et al.'s phases, and would be used to enhance the two processes.

Second, you have identified the culminating activities for the unit, the authentic assessments toward which all other activities are pointing; they also represent the essential questions for the unit (Wiggins & McTighe, 2005). All students are not expected to learn everything "taught" in the unit *but* each teen is expected to have much a better answer to the essential question at the end than she or he had at the outset of the unit.

Third, you may have noticed that every one of the twenty activities is written with the students think-work in mind, stating what the teens will be doing. Some of these activities may be difficult or unproductive for some students—(e) listening to the three tapes of the speech, (o) doing a word search, and (n) listening to the teacher (even for five minutes) are examples. Moreover, not every activity is worth doing—I am especially fond of dumping items (q) the multiple choice test (it only serves to stratify the grades) and (o) the word search (which I think wastes valuable class time). Interestingly some of the activities may be productive when done more than once; examples are (a) drafting their own questions and (k) a sharing experience.

No matter—each activity tells what kids do, making it easier to judge their relative value as part of a coherent learning experience.

Fourth, some readers have started to seek examples of the ENGAGING factors in the planned activities of the unit. Items (l), (k), and (r) may call for the use of graphic organizers, items (g) and (k) seek to motivate by building community, and items (b), (l), (m), and (r) help teens negotiate meaning and make their own notes. Moreover, although it is not explicitly stated, many of the activities can be done in collaborative structures. Finally, there is no indication of how the teacher will *grade* students in this unit, so there is still hope that grading will be done wisely.

Comparisons to Others

You now have a thoughtful sequence or flow of activities for your Pearl Harbor unit. Please keep it in mind as you read over the following narrative of others experiences.

Background

Two social studies teachers at Cheney High School have returned from a day-long professional development workshop on integrating "active" learning with both literacy and differentiation in the hopes of engaging their students. They are highly successful, highly dedicated, and creative veteran teachers. Driving back to the building from the workshop, they discuss the ideas they had been presented and mutually agree to experiment for the next week when they both begin a unit on Pearl Harbor. They agree to go to the Moose Hall next Friday at 5 PM to "compare notes" about their experimentation.

Here are the results of their individual explorations.

Mr. Bee

Mr. Bee is a very interesting eleventh grade social studies teacher. Despite his advancing age, he is passionate and enthusiastic in class at all times. He loves history; it makes him whole. He acts as if all the events and people he talks about—from Genghis Khan to weapons of mass destruction—affect him personally. He tells great and riveting stories (the one about Lee and Lincoln is his favorite) and he treats his students as if they were his own children. He is active in all school and community events. His classroom is full of artifacts that make it seem a little like a mini-Smithsonian. There are WWII helmets on the rack, posters from the National Geographic on the wall, maps (featuring countries that no longer exist!), and front pages of newspapers from key days in history. There are also about a dozen Jackdaw packets lying around the room (including Slavery, Holocaust, and Immigration), which are used for special investigations, extra credit, or as fillers when substitute teachers are in the room.

His multiple-choice tests are easy and many are open book; he also requires a few projects, which are very open ended and mostly of the group variety. He has relatively high grades and a 90% New York State Regents Examination passing rate.

As he contemplates the Pearl Harbor unit, he creates his plans this way:

Early: Bee wants the kids to have some useful background as they begin the unit, so he uses the first day to do the "basics": they find Pearl Harbor on the globe, they listen to him provide "six facts," the background knowledge they will need for a complete understanding. They record notes from the overhead notes on this presentation. He tells them about FDR's reaction and they hear one version of the infamy speech. They watch the clip from "Tora! Tora! Tora!," and for overnight homework they read six pages from the novel he provides. He starts day two by asking, "What did you think?," and they have a brief discussion. The students then read the textbook in class (taking notes). The last part of this day is taken up by students doing the word-search puzzle for the eight new terms.

Middle: Midweek classes are taken up with Bee explaining some of the finer points about the Pearl Harbor episode. He tells about the racist reaction by the U.S. people and their complete shock at being "attacked"; he makes sure the students know that this was the first time the United States had been attacked on its own soil since 1812…and he mentions that some folks believed that FDR helped "set it up." They listen to the rest of the "Infamy speeches" and actually read it aloud to each other in pairs; there was much excitement in their voices. He explains the pros and cons of the war vote in Congress and describes the nature of the alliances that brought *all* parties into the war. He assigns the rest of the chapter in the text for overnight reading and tells the kids that Friday's test will be "open notes."

Late: Thursday's class is used to have the students study for the test. Some read from the chapter, creating a good set of notes as they do. Others watch a film loop and study a Power Point presentation about the attack and its aftermath. Bee wanders the room, urging the kids to answer his favorite question, "See the point?" He does check people's notes for accuracy and he does tell a few more stories as he interacts with various groupings. Several times he notes that the text items in bold would make *good* test items. Several students use resources available in the room, including the stack of old NYS Regents Examinations, a set of library books on the table, the encyclopedia, and the posters. On Friday, the students take the twenty-five multiple-choice and one essay exam ("What were the causes and the effects of the events of December 7, 1941, a 'day of infamy'?"). Before they take the test, Bee tells the class that they could do extra credit over the weekend if they want. They can get up to a ten-point bonus if they either write some more test items (for other classes) or write a long reflection about the topic. They can get up to an additional twenty points if they create a five-page book called "Pearl Harbor: My View." They all understand and take the test individually and quietly. He also says that they will "go over the test" on Monday and use Tuesday as the "wrap-up."

Mr. Cee

Mr. Cee is considered a very engaging eleventh grade social studies teacher. He often frustrates the students by making them work for their own answers instead of telling them what he thinks, but for the most part, they learn to like that approach. Everyone knows that he answers a question with another question, but because they work in teams so often, most questions do receive a nod (if not directly answered). He is passionate about the United States and the idea of democracy: it is clear that he loves Jefferson (despite the slaves), Lincoln and FDR (they saved the country) and JFK (who gave the United States a postwar purpose), and thinks that the United States "could be something special in human history." He also gets excited when his students do what he calls "good thinking" and he tells them often that their ideas show great effort and are "brilliant" and "stand up to the evidence that they have so far." In truth, some Honors students think that he thinks way too highly of ordinary kids' ideas and they are resentful of the group work and the good grades that many students get in his classes. They do enjoy his challenges to them, however, and are always proud of their own efforts for him. His room is full of stuff, but the students themselves are responsible for the displays, so the posters and the papers are almost all student-made or designed.

Almost all of his grades come from student projects: "store-bought" multiple-choice tests are used as collaborative discussion tools (and he doesn't provide the answer keys). He has about a 90% passing rate on the New York State Regents Examination.

As he contemplates his Pearl Harbor unit, he makes his plans this way:

Early: The first day of the unit is always special for Cee. He wants to excite the students and connect to the issues of the unit, and he wants them to create a personal meaning for the upcoming content. On day one, they start by doing a "word acrostic" on the phrase S U R P R I S E A T T A C K. Students work alone, then in pairs. The large group debriefing reveals that students connect words like the following to a surprise attack: enraged, confused, tricked, ambushed, killed, ugly, retaliate. These were written on butcher block paper and hung at the front of the classroom. Cee tells the class that come next Monday, "Let's see how these words did connect to the events of December 7, 1941, the surprise attack by the Japanese on the United States at Pearl Harbor."

As he finishes speaking, twelve hands are in the air, indicating that students have something to say about the issue. Cee immediately puts them in their regular pairs (cross-gender partners, for the most part) and tells them to list eight things they know about Pearl Harbor. After a brief whole-class sharing (and one quick look at the map and pictures on p. 978 in the text), Cee asks the class, "What seems important or essential to know about this event?" Students work to develop a list of six personal questions they have, then use a scavenger hunt to see what other kids wrote. Eventually, a list of four questions everybody has to answer and a personalized list of four more is created, forming the heart of the project due Friday: a five-page book called "Pearl Harbor: My View."

Middle: During the middle of the week, events vary in class. Some time is used for students to work on their books and some time is used for them to share in pairs and in teams the ideas and inferences they were making. Class work is stopped several times for specific activities for all to do—they watch and comment on a clip from Tora! Tora! Tora!; they read and draw illustrations for a brief passage from a novel; they read and write elaboration questions from a passage in the text (Cee answered many of them and put others on the board); they evaluate a set of questions made by another class; they make a T-bar of reasons for and against a congressional declaration of war (Cee warns them about alliances but each class supports a yes vote); and they listen to FDR's "Infamy speech" as if they were Japanese military leaders. (This sparks a heated whole-class discussion as some students are angry that others can "take an anti-U.S. perspective"). At the end of each day (Tuesday through Thursday) the students complete in writing a brief *outslip*, choosing from these items:

 ◆ Today I learned that…

- One way that I helped others today was…
- I still wonder about …
- The reason today's work was important is …
- People should realize that Pearl Harbor represents…

Late: Cee uses Friday as a "total-work" day, telling the students that their actual books are not due as finished products until Tuesday, but that half of their project grade will be determined by the end of class Friday. Class time is spent conferencing with each student, assessing what they are planning, offering ideas and suggestions, nixing bad designs, negotiating new directions, inspiring efforts, and editing products. He suggests that they work over the weekend and plan to use Monday to finish, but also tells them that a few minutes on Monday will be used to take a simulated test on the topic.

Something interesting happens in Friday's class: the students demand that the generic project rubric that they have been using all year be amended and modified for this specific project. For example, what does he mean by "book?" What does he mean by "five pages?" What does "spelling counts" mean? Substantial time is taken on Friday and the result is a five-item, four-level rubric for the project. The elements included the following:

- accuracy
- depth and breadth of content
- use of conventions
- creativity
- use of evidence

Please use the Venn diagram in the space below to record your comparison of the two men to each other (and/or to you).

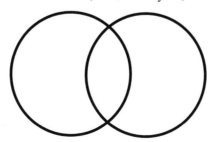

Are you ready for a third member of the department? The next passage is about Mr. Dee.

Mr. Dee

Mr. Dee is the third, aging, male, veteran social studies teacher at Cheney. He, too, has been there since he got his BA in history and geography from State back in the late 1970s. He knows Bee and Cee very well, having worked in the department with them for a long time; they had worked together on departmental issues for a while, but then seemed to drift apart. (Interestingly, when they were younger they all served as assistant football coaches for a three-year period). Mr. Dee didn't go to the workshop, but overheard the discussions in the faculty room. When he heard that the other two were going to try some new ideas, he perked up. Although he did not read any of the materials lying around the faculty room coffee table, he did have a lunch conversation with a female student teacher from the nearby college. He thought that the novice's ideas were basically unworkable and that she was also too idealistic. Mr. Dee was convinced that students are essentially lazy, don't care about their own educations, are rude, self-centered, and "disasters waiting to happen." Although he had doubts, he, too, planned a new unit on Pearl Harbor.

In general, students and parents don't mind Dee as a teacher. He doesn't push too hard on assignments, gives easy tests, and his classes aren't "bad," just boring. They think that his stories are pretty funny and they think that history is literally "his story"! His room has many posters of Americana and his love for the Civil War is shown by all the toys, statues, and relics that he has strewn around the room.

If they study hard from May on, they'll do fine on the State exams, except for the few low-ability students that slip through the administration filters and end up in his class. (These are generally minority teens and they don't have much clout or voice in school.)

> *Early:* Mr. Dee is genuinely concerned that the students will not have any context to help them remember the key things about Pearl Harbor, so he spends about twenty minutes on the first day giving them notes. He uses the front board to provide an outline and then talks, just like college history teachers do. They take a few minutes to read the captions and look at three pictures in the text. He comments on how they show the real truth of how gruesome it was for "us to be attacked." He also indicates that this attack was laying the groundwork for Hiroshima and Nagasaki and for the United States to be ever suspicious of Asian nations. Over the first three days, the students also see about thirty minutes of "Tora! Tora! Tora!,"

write answers to the text chapter-ending questions during class, and listen to two stories about surviving veterans who had returned to the local town as scarred and damaged young men.

Middle: During the middle of the unit, Mr. Dee tries to make his new unit more student-centered by having the kids go to the library and do some research on any "aspect" of the event that they want. He quickly concludes that this is a waste of time, as only sixteen of his 125 students actually start doing meaningful work. As he watches them flounder in the library for the entire period, he is heard to mutter something about how they "are doomed to failure at college." Mr. Dee does tell several classes about two of his friends who flunked out of college as freshmen because they didn't know how to research anything and he suggests that they start taking school seriously.

Late: Now concerned that they hadn't learned anything substantial about the incident, Mr. Dee invents a new task, one that combines the test with the facts of the event. Throwing out his old exam, he tells each period that they are going to design their own tests. "You certainly should pass the test, when you make the questions!" he bellows. The groups of three work two periods to make the items. He doesn't tell them, but Mr. Dee plans to use the items written by first period for the next class, and alternate until each class has a different test and one that others have made up. Students make many questions of the "What time did it start?" and "Who ordered the attack?" variety and the scores on the test average about 47%. Three of the Honors students get below 70% and are outraged—they think he has abdicated his responsibility. He offers them a chance to make up 25 points (each) by watching the rest of "Tora! Tora! Tora!" and writing two pages about its historical accuracy. The experience of trying to engage the students leaves Mr. Dee disappointed, frustrated, and even more convinced of the decadence of contemporary adolescent scholarship. He is a little angry with Bee and Cee as well, and rejects their offers to visit their classrooms to see their innovations in operation. As a final gesture, Mr. Dee takes fifteen minutes one night to write the principal, complaining that the "new, student-centered stuff didn't work" and asking for money to buy two new filmstrips on Pearl Harbor and a class set of review books to prepare the teens for the New York State Regents Examination.

Author's Comments

Frankly, I dislike the approach of Mr. Dee; he appears to be counting on the students to learn most of their history at home (when they "study"). Not much of value is happening in his classes.

Mr. Bee is fairly traditional; he offers information first and then tries to direct student attention to "practice it." He is very fearful of any type of discussion until (some) of the students have enough "background knowledge." Most students work hard enough to gain the ideas, but some are lost and unable to connect new information to their prior knowledge.

Mr. Cee is a constructivist, working from student experience and knowledge and adding new ideas as they are genuinely sought or needed by students. His use of "outslips" helps students track their own thinking and they do have much ownership of their own meaning making.

While I clearly think that Mr. Cee is the furthest along the ENGAGING path, perhaps the best thing we can do here is to ask you to reskim the passages to answer these eight questions (called "ENGAGING spotting"). They should help you reflect on the work you're envisioned and move you toward my understanding of good teaching.

Spotting the ENGAGING Process

E entice effort by building relationships and encouraging often

N negotiate their own meanings

G group for collaboration

A active learning and active [authentic] assessment

G graphic organizers to force conceptual connections

I intelligence interventions to make diversities strengths

N note making (not note taking)

G grade wisely

♦ How has the instructor tried to build relationships with students *and* foster a sense of community in the classroom?

♦ How has the instructor tried to force learners to develop their own understandings of important concepts and practices?

- How has the instructor used grouping to build collaboration among students?

- How has the instructor promoted active learning and used differentiated authentic assessments to help learners think deeply about the content?

- How has the instructor utilized graphic organizers to help students think deeply about ideas *and/or* document their own insights?

- How has the instructor utilized "[multiple] intelligences theory" and "spontaneous interventions" to promote quality work *and* to make diversity a strength?

- How have students been asked to record their own thinking, personalize their own thinking, and develop understandings during class time *and* during reading assignments?

- How has this instructor's grading policy contributed to student motivation, students' sense of accomplishment, student level of interest, and a sense of community?

How to Teach Well:
Detailing and Exemplifying the Eight Factors

Enticing Effort by Building
Relationships and Fostering Community

A few years ago the National Association of Secondary School Principals (NASSP) sponsored a series of research studies using the "shadow technique." At numerous cites around the country on the same day, researchers studied the day being spent at a school by a specific teen. The authors gathered the data and looked for patterns. One of the most interesting findings they uncovered was a simple truth that is painfully obvious to anyone who talks to teens or who watches teaching: students spend most of their days sitting quietly watching and (maybe) listening as a teacher talks, a movie runs, or maybe staring at the words in their texts. School is boring, it is irrelevant, and it demands no sense of personal examination or use of ideas. In the ninth grade study, they also discovered that the average student spoke publicly once every day in class and then only for a short period (as in a word like "yes").

ENGAGEMENT seems to be the antithesis of that kind of passive and deadly inaction. And it is.

With active learning comes a strange truth that has yet to be discovered by many teachers: When asked to have an original thought, most students most often actually have something powerful to say or valuable to add to class dialogue and are capable of integrating ideas. Taught in a constructivist, ENGAGING manner, teens will make new, interesting sense out of important content.

But along with good thinking comes a fascinating hypothesis: When taught that way, students' ideas are essential to a class as they become the raw material of the lesson. Student ideas make everyone interdependent on each other, and they result in students feeling valued, respected, and necessary. This, of course, means that they matter.

Most readers of this book already have a set of strategies to help them connect with teens: use their names, go to their events, ask them about their interests, look at their clothes, and watch who they hang with. Teachers have stood by their classroom doors for decades, chatting up the students as they enter or leave. All of this is good and extremely valuable, but what I am offering here are some ideas about building relationships with teens *during* instruction: teaching in a way that puts the individual student's ideas at the forefront of the lesson.

I advocate teaching from a loosely coupled model developed by Flynn et al. (2004) called the Two-Step (see Chapter 3 for a review of this process and, if you wish, you can reflect on its operation in the previous section on Pearl Harbor). The first step, the Exploratory, essentially revolves around getting every student ready to do meaningful work. If you know Hunter's (1982) anticipatory set, you know you have to "hook" them; but her quick, one-size-fits-all one-minute opening seldom touches all students, rarely, if ever, calls up sufficient prior knowledge for each student, and even more rarely gives the student a chance to receive public recognition for an idea or accomplishment. The Exploratory is a deliberate step to fix those shortcomings and has the side benefit of allowing every student to personalize his or her readiness.

The second step, called the Discovery, involves the production of meaningful demonstrations of understanding by every student. Literally, Flynn et al. mean that students work and produce evidence, some real thing that can be assessed, that shows what students understand. These two phases demand that students cannot slip through the cracks offered by teachers when they send work home or when they expect students to learn at home or outside the classroom. In this model, the applicable metaphor is a "workshop" and the participating students are the think-workers.

The value to relationship building and the fostering of community in the Two-Step model is enormous. Students are now often parts of teams who are planning, creating, and sharing their products. (This is just like the adult world of valuable well-paying work, according to many, including Friedman [2005].) Student ideas are valued because they are necessary to content understanding and assessment is built into the learning process, making it continuous and ongoing. Failures can only happen if the teacher *cannot* motivate the individual student to *try* during class time.

Here are a few "slightly different" strategies that can help develop the willingness to "try" within a class period; they are compared to more traditional practices. (These examples have been drawn from lessons that I have taught in real settings. Each worked to involve every student.)

To begin a learning experience (Exploratory)

Eighth graders were asked to make a T-bar showing aspects of good and bad bosses and share them with neighbors. Discussions ensued about how bosses can take advantage of their workers. (This was tied to good and bad governmental leaders and eventually to the need for the Bill of Rights.)

Seventh graders were asked to list enjoyable rides that they know from carnivals and to share what was fun about them. They also had to spot any dangerous parts. (This was used to offer analogies for the digestive system of humans and became a model for a theme park ride that represented this system.)

Eleventh graders were asked to list everything that they knew about war and build categories for their ideas with neighbors. (Eventually they used their own categories to plan a museum exhibit on the Korean War.)

Ninth graders were given a set of written descriptions and were asked to choose several and draw what the short paragraphs meant. (These became the diagrams for math problems built on the premise that creating visuals is helpful in understanding the demands of the word problem and the interrelationships of ideas.)

In every case, students could not be wrong with their first ideas (which were recorded on paper and shared with classmates). Teachers and peers often praised others' ideas, respected the efforts, and borrowed some of them. Instead of receiving teacher information, students were building their own knowledge and preparing themselves to integrate their existing schema with the new ideas that were inevitably coming from the next step in the process.

As the year wears on, students have more and better ideas and teachers know more and increasingly interesting things about the teens as individuals. This unveiling process is phenomenally powerful in helping make the students seem human and respectable…and individuals. People who tutor and those who have interacted with their own children know this process intimately; they use it all the time. When asked by a respected adult who is really curious, "What do you think?," it is difficult for a teen to not respond and to not feel positive affect for the other person and for the (learning) situation.

When creating meaning/completing the task (Discovery)

Ninth grade students were asked to create menus for a new Spanish restaurant, using a list of mandated words for entrees and vegetables.

Eighth grade students were asked to write and sing a song that identifies the steps in solving quadratic equations.

Seventh graders were asked to create a set of skits called "Discovering the New World" from the perspectives of various (ethnic) groups of people.

Tenth graders were asked to design a set of visuals to include in the next edition of Orwell's *1984*.

Eleventh graders were asked to design and do a presentation/workshop for fourth graders called "the basics of chemistry," which is to be videotaped and shown to the school board as well.

Each of these active and authentic tasks can be seen as motivating and differentiated in its own right. These two factors alone produce a great deal of motivation for most teens. But one other factor seeps through and should be noticed: As students spend class time working on these products, the teacher can engage different students in different discussions about different aspects of the various jobs. These dialogues show interest in the individual, are personalized, and almost always give opportunities for praise of work and/or effort; they are far less likely to be concentrated on just "fixing" a mistake than the regular guided practice session usually does. They spark ingenuity and creativity and focus on student strengths, making teachers and students aware of successes and abilities. It is motivating to have someone find something good about you and your effort. For a teen, this process may also result in the student gaining appreciation for the teacher and a deeper commitment to school (see Fredericks, Blumenfeld, & Paris, 2004).

Over the long run, the sheer number of identifiable positives for any one student would be staggering and their impact on attitude and collective impact on classroom atmosphere would be enormous. A sense of trust develops as well, so when corrections must come or modifications are called for, the student sees the teacher as an ally, *not* as a boss. The metaphor for the role of "coach" jumps out in this context. We don't often see the coach as prison guard or evaluator. More likely, the coach is seen as advocate and facilitator for a person trying to get better at something important.

When the student owns his or her work, the teacher becomes a helper and an assistant to the teen's overall growth. This type of encouraging and supportive role has been largely lost in U.S. classrooms (but not playing fields) since enactment of *No Child Left Behind* (NCLB).

I do urge you to stand in the door, ask students about their lives, and go to the plays, dances, spaghetti dinners, and games. But also please consider using those 900 classes a year as opportunities to build community, sustain relationships, forge interactions that are respectful and satisfying, and to have teens examine and create ideas in their own unique ways.

Negotiate Meanings

The second factor of the ENGAGING process is the key one from a cognitive (learning) perspective: Recognize that students need to make their own understandings of important content and that they are going to do so anyway. Let me first be practical and then theoretical about this important point.

Mark the following true or false.

_____ 1. If you fall asleep at 11 and take a two-hour nap, you awake at 1.

_____ 2. If you add 11 + 2, you get 13.

_____ 3. The U.S.A. is the greatest country in human history.

_____ 4. An adult female human cannot get pregnant if she has sexual intercourse while standing.

_____ 5. The key point in the book 1984 is that governments lie.

_____ 6. The U.S. Civil War was about race and slavery.

_____ 7. The United States had no choice—it had to nuke Japan.

_____ 8. In a vacuum, heavier objects fall faster than lighter objects.

These items were intended to be a bit whacky, but I say "thank you" for trying to answer them. For at least a few, you probably felt an urge to write your reasoning in the margin (or send it to my e-mail, pjv@niagara.edu). The truth is that for almost all learning in secondary schools, the reasons behind the thinking are more important than the answers generated (in other words, process trumps product). However, traditional schooling has paid scant attention to that truth.

My practical advice is to recognize that a student's current take on the content cries out for a chance to explain the position, to examine it against evidence or argument, and prepare to modify or tweak beliefs in the future. You cannot force a student to believe your truths; only his or her truths make sense. There is much evidence of this fact; they can give the teacher the "right answer" and maintain different (original) beliefs without losing sleep or changing their minds! Thus, teachers should help them establish their own beliefs and have them consider ways to change their minds if (and when) necessary.

You might not want the answer key, but here it goes anyway: (1) and (2) seem to be true, although paradoxical; (3) is an opinion seen as a fact by many of us here in the U.S.A. (This is not seen as true across the globe, however. Canadians often mark this item differently.) My grandmother thought (4) was true (and may have been wrong), and my friend Greg thinks (5) is true. But, then again, Greg thinks all real governments lie, too. Historians argue to this day about (6); (7) is found in old "history" textbooks, so it must be true; (8) is false, but most of us believe it to be true anyway. I really wish that I could have been privy to your thinking during the test and while you were processing my version of the "answers."

Practically speaking, all of this means that the students must test and retest their own developing knowledge base frequently. Getting the answer right is far less important than is doing the thinking to resolve the confusions inherent in knowledge that is inert and/or irrelevant.

Theoretically speaking, this call to negotiate meaning is a wonderful opportunity to force teens to establish what they know and force them to spend some time finding and evaluating evidence for their beliefs. Putting ideas into "their own words" is one step in the right direction, and having students find support to defend their answers is another. School thus shifts from the dissemination of a lot of semitruths to the thoughtful study of a couple of big and important ideas. In the latter case, the study is done by the teen; in the former case, the dissemination is done by the teacher.

By the way, knowledge is internal; it is what is inside a student's mind (no matter its objective "quality" as true or false). Information is external, but it is of little value outside of a specific person's mind. This leads to one of the troubling aspects of traditional schooling: students need to be correct/accurate only 65% of the time, given our reliance on multiple-guess tests. Apparently in traditional school, one-third of a teen's beliefs can be mush (or pure gibberish) and he or she can still be thought of as a marginally competent person. UGH!

To close out this section on student construction of knowledge, we should examine truths that are interpretations by thinkers and those that are considered to be accurate by the testing done by the disciplines that form secondary schooling. Most of the important questions are ones of interpretation, ones that are not easily amenable to multiple choice tests and ones that demand student explanations. Thoughtful answers to these questions mark the old term "the educated man." They involve thought and judgment and help shape a teen's developing worldview.

In the other category are the factual truths developed by the disciplines; some of these are important, but they are more valuable on the *Jeopardy!* TV show than to a committed citizen-worker in a democracy. They do fit nicely on true/false tests but are of little use except in defending a judgment question, or an interpretation. In truth, facts are best thought of as "evidence" for generalized understandings.

Let students generate their own meanings and beliefs and then defend them with evidence; teens will grow cognitively and affectively from that kind of education.

Group Collaboratively

When the famous brothers, Roger and David Johnson, began their scholarly investigations into the use of Cooperative Learning in the early 1980s, education was mostly seen as a private experience done by an individual sitting amongst twenty or so others in a room at a given time. Assignments and projects, thought to be places where private minds could expand and grow, were almost all done alone. Competition between individuals, usually in the form of bell-curved tests, was perceived to be the most successful philosophy.

Boy, have times changed. Today, thanks to tireless advocacy, modeling in the business community, and a huge research base, cooperation reigns. Every new teacher must have some kind of group work thing in his or her "bag of tricks" to bring out at the interview, and actual collaboration on student projects is commonplace. A walk through the halls of a high school may still reveal a plethora of frontal teacher talk to rows of quiet receivers, but no one would be surprised to see the occasional groups of students doing actual think work, or small pairs working on some problem or two.

Today, we group for collaboration. The research support on this topic is overwhelmingly positive and, although some teachers cannot find it in their hearts to work this way, most teachers use it, and will use it more often in the future.

Chapter 4 provides a substantial reanalysis of how to make groups work effectively, but in this section I want to offer a few bromides to get you started. The entire ENGAGING process is embedded in collaboration, so it works as motivator, social and emotional context, intellectual spark, feedback provider and as a laboratory for teen work/life preparation.

Listening to the teacher explain answers to questions not felt or reading passages about uninteresting topics are poor ways to get students to be intrinsically motivated to think deeply. Giving them rewards like pizzas only cheapens the effort and actually works as a demotivator (Bain, 2004). However, real dialogue with real classmates exchanging their real ideas certainly should make class more interesting and clearly makes the time in class go by much faster.

Putting students to work—exchanging, comparing, creating and *not* copying answers—puts each individual in the middle of his or her own meaning making and defeats all the problems with cookie-cutter, one-size-fits-all, large-group presentations. Respectful collaboration can become a philosophy of how we are to act with others in our neighborhoods and at our jobs and teenagers can develop these skills and attitudes while thinking deeply. The teens should be forced to think deeply about issues of interaction, respectfulness, empathy, and tolerance—while experiencing and reflecting about it!

Collaboration motivates by offering teens some challenges or reinforcements for their ideas; by making their thinking stand up to public examination; by making it safe to try out new ideas and change one's mind often; and by contributing to the overall social good while developing concepts.

Spencer Kagan (1992) developed an entire set of user-friendly and simple "structures" by which students can be activated in class. He adapted Frank Lyman's "think-pair-share" and created others such as "four corners," but each of these is designed to make the learner (a) create an idea and communicate it, (b) handle feedback on the idea from a respected other (Mesibov, 2003), (c) consider and assess new possibilities, and (d) make the learner become thoughtfully aware of what the learner thinks and believes. Each strategy is set up so it can be done by any student at any time—so they have universal qualities. Strategies that expect students to speak their ideas to others and to consider their responses makes the work in the classroom relevant, purposeful, and, frankly, more enjoyable.

Done well and often enough, Cooperative Learning is something that every teen will appreciate, even if it results in the student having to think more and work harder; the social context, like that on a sports team, will provide norms of contribution and participation, and students will gladly choose schooling with that type of meaning making over the contemporary model. The competitive, go-it-alone model can continue to shrink toward oblivion.

I close this section with a few caveats that should be taken seriously.

♦ Do *not* assume that students know what collaboration looks like or how to do it. Be ready to discuss expectations and interpersonal skills and to demonstrate them. The "how to cooperate" skills should be taught, monitored, assessed, and reflected upon by both teacher and students. Students also need to reflect on how they actually act during sharing activities which is critical and, unfortunately, the most likely aspect of Cooperative Learning to be ignored.

♦ Beware of the *one-does-it model:* this is the common practice of three students waiting for a fourth student to do *all* the work. As many teachers continue to use lower-Bloom-level activities and questions for their teams, students gain no cognitive advantage by working together. If there is no analysis, no synthesis, and no exchange of ideas, there is no need for teamwork. Students simply wait for one to do the job and then copy the answers from her or him. (And if they are group-graded, *pass* the test or complete the project. There is no learning in such a structure; just copying).

♦ Teams don't learn, even when they finish assigned jobs. Teams work so that individuals learn. Make sure that each student is assessed separately for his or her understanding *after* a teamwork session. This means at least part of the grading plan must take into account each individual's gain, whether in the cognitive or the affective domain. Many of us also ignore this aspect of Cooperative Learning.

Active Learning and Active, Authentic Assessment

Take a quick quiz:

1. Would you rather listen to a lecture or converse with another person?

2. Would you rather watch people play a game or play it yourself?

3. Would you prefer to make some predictions or watch others make some?

4. Would you prefer to look silently at a work of art or tell your impressions about it to someone else?

5. Would you prefer to choose a song to listen to or let someone else pick?

6. Would you rather take a multiple-choice test (and be marked) or orally explain your answers in detail?

7. Would you rather think about a passage you're reading or simply let your eyes pass over it ?

Now, I am not sure what exactly to do with your answers but the test serves as a springboard for some comments about active learning; most of the time, active engagement is the preferred mode *and* leads to better understanding of new ideas. The more engaged we are in processing information, making sense of an experience (reflection) and in communicating it to someone else, the deeper the understanding (and the more permanent the memory).

Chapter 3 presents "convincing" scholarly evidence that this is true, but I would like to use this section to show you some examples of how to turn passive reception into active processing, with the likelihood of higher test scores as one likely result.

- ♦ Instead of lecturing on the six causes of the War, Mr. Vermette gives out a handout listing the six causes *and* asks the students to discuss and write an explanation of *why* each fact would lead to war. Later, they compare their hypotheses (explanations) with the material in the book and on the Internet.

- ♦ Instead of doing a demo at the board to show how to add two expressions $(x^2 + 3x - 7)$ and $(-5x^2 - 37x + 14)$, Ms. Jones asks the student teams to develop three ways to add them. The solutions are discussed by the entire class.

- ♦ In physics, Mr. Bower asks the class to design a way to use a balance beam, thirty small objects, and a scale to devise a formula about equalities.

- ♦ In Spanish, Senora Kline asks the students to examine a word list containing thirty-five new items and asks them to guess about the meanings of them. After ten minutes, they look them up and rate their predictions.

- ♦ In math, Mr. Johnston hands out three solved problems based on yesterday's work. He announces that there are mistakes in the solutions in each and challenges the students to identify and explain them. The students work in pairs.

- ♦ In social studies, Mr. Wright hands out a list of so-called rights and asks the students if they are a right protected by law. Examples include the following:

  #3: A young black male student at a crowded party starts berating a white male student and uses racial slurs;

  #7: At 3 AM a car comes down the quiet and secluded street blaring its radio as loud as possible to the hip-hop station;

  #13: A female student is stopped by a counselor in front of her homeroom and is told to open her purse and empty her pockets because they are looking for drugs and she is a "likely candidate."

At the end of class, each student will write his or her opinion *and* compare it to the opinions of the justices in the U.S. Supreme Court case analogous to each scenario.

"Minds-on" trumps "hands-on" activity. The principle of "the more directly active the processing of the information, the deeper the understanding" should also be modified to suggest that it is the thinking about the material that matters, *not* the activity of the hands. Creation of a new integration of ideas, the use of evidence to support a decision, and/or the solving of a problem all lead to cognitive (schema) change *and* (new) learning. Having the students manipulate the material personally and intentionally, and preferably, audibly and visibly, are clearly engaging and effective practices.

Through the past few years, I have challenged my Methods of Teaching classes at Niagara University to complete this statement: "Lecture doesn't work unless _____." I hope that you tried a few words in the blank and thought about how they sounded. If not, do so now, please. Here are some common phrases offered:

- ◆ "Unless the student is making notes about his or her understandings."

- ◆ "Unless the information being offered has been sought by the student(s)."

- ◆ "Unless the teacher asks some questions or asks for reactions to the ideas after a short period of time."

- ◆ "Unless the teacher has the students turn to a partner and summarize what was said."

These responses sound reasonable to many of us; the lecture itself is just information, but if it is processed by the student, it will be better understood and become some form of knowledge for the learner.

Active learning is seldom openly challenged anymore but one does hear teachers talk about "students *absorbing* the new ideas" (although parents and laypeople use that metaphor all the time, too. I wish that all of us would start talking about students "integrating" new ideas, and forgo the passive language). The problem with the active learning principle is that it is often forgotten when secondary teachers are faced with a time crunch, a coverage overload and/or a piece of content that they don't know well. Ironically, when something is new and unfamiliar, learners' time, focus, and energy must be put into playing with it, examining it and thinking about it—and neither teachers nor students tend to do that. Superficial rehearsal seems to raise its ugliest head with the new and complex content that most needs an investment of thoughtful engagement.

Active learning also leads to active authentic assessment; the teacher should ask himself/herself: "What do I want them to understand?" *and* "What will they produce to demonstrate their understanding?" Doing this often leads to a simplistic but powerful alignment between the objective (in some places called *performance indicators, outcomes,* or *goals*) and the assessment instrument.

As you read these objectives, try to create a vision of a student showing, describing, or exhibiting something to you that clearly demonstrates that the student understands what is being sought.

1. Explain the processes by which an animal digests food.

2. Explain the connection between multiplication and addition.

3. Solve problems that utilize the Pythagorean theorem.

4. Compare capitalism and communism as economic structures.

5. Create a metaphor for the steps to the Civil War.

6. Compare and contrast the concepts of theme and setting in a real short story.

7. Choose a complete meal from a French-language menu.

While there are numerous possibilities for each (and in my classes, I do not allow a true/false or multiple-guess question to serve as an assessment), each of those possibilities requires a tangible product and most likely requires a verbal explanation of it. Thus, the assessment becomes an active and visible process. Moreover, at least some of the class time between the stating of the objectives and the finishing of the product should be used in the process of developing an answer. Far too often all the real processing is done at home.

For example, in goal 4 above, a discussion in class should offer ideas for student use, and should help direct student thinking, and offer feedback on thinking attempts. (The discussions in different classes may take different directions but they are all driven by the same objective.) In goal 3 above, it is pretty obvious that students will spend some time in class solving some problems and explaining their thinking.

To summarize, when the objective aligns well with the authentic assessment, and there is thoughtful linkage between the two, class time can be productively spent helping learners make the connection and reflecting on their attempts at completing the challenge.

Intelligence Interventions

By now the educational community has taken Howard Gardner's theory of multiple intelligences to heart and uses it as a rationale for many decisions (even some he may disagree with). As he sees it, intelligence is many things (eight to be exact) and they present ways of solving problems or fashioning products that use constellations of qualities that are diverse across individuals. To confuse you (just a little more), I can rephrase this point to say that "intelligences are many things." Gardner does not think of intelligence as a singular entity, but as a set of distinct qualities, each worthy of the title "intelligence." The implications of this point, not often thoroughly realized, are that there are (at least) eight ways of being smart, eight ways to finish a task, eight ways to demonstrate understanding, eight ways to be aroused to thought, and so forth. (By the way, Gardner would say that "intelligences are" *not* "intelligence is." Again, the implications of his notion of plural equivalent abilities is often ignored.) In short, when kids are working on showing their understandings, they will need fruitful interventions by the teacher (or other students) and these interventions can take a myriad of forms. Choosing of the forms could be random but selection by an intentional choice drawn from multiple intelligences theory may prove to be more productive in the long run.

Here are some examples:

♦ A math student is having trouble making sense of a narrative in his text so the teacher asks him to create a flowchart showing the key steps.

♦ A biology teacher asks her entire class to think of mitosis as a series of important operations and asks them to think of particular music that each step is similar to.

♦ An English teacher asks her students to pick a character in a short story and imagine the character meeting someone from class and talking about a situation from the story, and act it out for the entire class.

♦ A social studies student who is working on a biography of Churchill has trouble understanding Churchill's complex personality. The teacher asks her to write some sentences as if she were an opponent of Churchill.

Although the exact matching of intelligence with intervention is impossible (because verbal linguistic is involved in everything done in schools), I'd suggest that visual–spatial, musical–rhythmic, body–kinesthetic, and interpersonal intelligences guided the four interventions in the examples above.

By realizing that interventions are important both as feedback *and* thinking with eight kinds of smart, the teacher recognizes that there are a variety of ways to assist in every case, and is encouraged by the differentiated range of possible courses of action. Moreover, respecting the intelligences also opens up multiple ways to assess authentic achievement, and opens the door for choice theory (as Glasser [1986] may have wanted it.)

To summarize, differentiation, the current great hope of reaching *every* teen, is exacerbated by the use of authentic tasks tied to choice and open to multiple intelligences forms and structures.

Note Making Versus Note Taking

In what may seem to be the simplest and easiest strategy to use, note making, teachers have to remember that their "coverage" of material does not align very well with student "understanding" of it. Teachers, who present information, do just that: they offer it, as a Power Point presentation, in reading, or in verbal form. There is no reason to believe that most of the kids receive the information as the teacher meant for it to be received. Once again, the metaphor of "absorbing" ideas is a disaster as a model for learning; it is the ENGAGEMENT that the student actively and thoughtfully does to, or with, the information that makes it his or her own and which fosters an understanding—and *every* one of these is unique to an individual. Constructivist theory recognizes that the student must develop conceptual understanding for himself, and that approach *does not* just call for remembering.

Let's play for a minute with four examples that may help us contextualize the point made above.

1. Following this statement is another statement, drawn from some 1970s U.S. history books. Please study it until you can recite it perfectly three times without looking. Once you have it, go to the next item: "The United States had no choice—it had to 'nuke' Japan."

Are you ready to go on?

2. This item deals with that most difficult subject, math. To divide fractions, you must remember the rule, "invert the divisor and multiply." It seems pretty simple, but, like most math, it is difficult for many students. Try your hand at these sample problems, while using the rule:

    a. $2/3 \div 1/2 =$

    b. $4/5 \div 7/8 =$

    c. $6/4 \div 1/3 =$

    d. $1/10 \div 2 =$

    e. $4/9 \div 4/9 =$

    f. $.25 \div 1/2 =$

Commentary

If you can recite the "Japan" item, you have "learned" history as most of us remember: recitation, rehearsal, and meaningless gibberish ("study" meant "rehearse"). However, maybe you've tried to elaborate on it on your own—made a picture of it in your mind, generated arguments to disagree with it as you say it; wondered where the statement came from; wondered about Japanese-American kids' reactions to it. Maybe you've even reflected on what similar memory tasks you expect from your students. In any case, you were asked to remember it and "make note" of it. (In the old days, we might have been asked to write it 100 times to make sure that we have it "cold"!)

If learners were note making the way I am suggesting, very different processes would have been invoked. For example, consider students doing each of the following:

- ◆ Write a reaction sentence as if you were Ichiro, a Japanese-American teenager in a Detroit school, when he reads this statement in a text.

- ◆ Name three sources of information that might support or refute the premise of the statement. (*Note:* This is what many liberal arts historians would want the teens to be doing.)

- ◆ Ask the students to complete these four statements:

  1. To the Japanese, the bombing of Hiroshima meant...

  2. One reason some Americans might want to believe that "no choice" statement is true is that...

  3. One "choice" that the United States could have considered was...

  4. When I realize that the only nation in history to use "atomic" weapons on human beings was the United States, I feel...

In all three of these thoughtful activities, students are asked to think about the statement and make notes about their own thinking. The notes they make, like the ones you might have written in above, represent their own understanding and are great cues to recall and to deeper understanding. They assume an active and competent human being and demand that students take charge of their own educations. Moreover, unlike simple memory work, these are the types of cognitive activities that smart people actually do. Moreover, the fourth completion item called for an affective response, a powerful strategy for increasing motivation and ownership (Kline & Vermette, 2006;

Glasser, 1986). Smart people also use intra-personal and interpersonal intelligences (Goleman, 2006; Gardner, 1983, 2006).

Let's try this approach to documenting right now. These next items attempt to force you into note making. (By the way, some of you have already written your own comments in the margins of this text; that is an active response *and* an example of note making!)

Here are a couple of examples:

1. One way that note making differs from note taking is....

2. One reason that my students might feel positive about making their own notes is....

3. In the space below, briefly tell which of the author's three initial examples makes the most sense to you and why.

Turn for a moment now to the division by fractions quiz that you took a few minutes ago.

Chances are that you got the right answer on this math quiz. However, it is very telling where you stopped *and* had to "troubleshoot" the rule a little. For example, did you understand that 2 is actually 2/1, so the rule can be used? What did you think dividing by ½ actually means? Most of us think it is the same as dividing by 2; can you draw a picture visually showing what the question is asking? Can you think of a real-life situation that aligns with the numbers offered in the example?

Note making would force the students to answer these questions (and have the response documented in writing), generate and answer a few more of their own (a form of KWL), and perhaps allow a think-pair-share in which students see and comment on each others' thoughts.

Teaching math by heuristic is different than teaching it conceptually. The first approach suggests that successful application drills in deep understanding: $2/3 \div 4/5$ is the same as $2/3 \times 5/4$ which equals $10/12$, reduced to $5/6$. Right? Right! But I doubt that hundreds of successful applications would allow the learner to grasp the meaning of the operation, the reason for the processes used, or possible uses for it in real life. The use of note making could force the idea generation and guide the conceptual clarifications necessary for meaning.

In short, note making is a way for students to document their own actual thinking about difficult content and includes their insights, their confusions, their developing generalizations, and, eventually, their (new) schemata.

3. Let's extend this idea of note making to the clarification of an important *concept*, the part of secondary content that is really at the heart of the curricula. Drawing from the ample literature that supports the use of nonexemplars to help clarify concep-

tual meaning (Bruner, 1996), the example below requires that you jot down your own reactions as called for.

For each of the following, explain why it is or is not, a *sentence*.

1. Bob got out of the chair and left for the store.
   Is it a sentence: why or why not?
2. When he got there, he asked, "Is it closed?"
   Is it a sentence: why or why not?
3. "Yes" came the reply from within.
   Is it a sentence: why or why not?
4. "OK."
   Is it a sentence: why or why not?
5. He left, puzzled: why was there an answer?
   Is it a sentence: why or why not?

After the students (you) write their answers, small groups share responses and then the whole class does. (You may have to find several friendly English teachers for feedback.) Finally, near the close of class, each student writes his or her own "description" of a sentence and what is needed for a group of words to be a sentence.

When done, the students have a record of their attempts and their final conclusion; these appear to be notes but they have not been "taken" traditionally. The process used was note making and it was genuine, authentic, personal, reflective, and ENGAGING.

4. Finally, let's examine a variant of another strategy called "guided notes." Almost always, guided notes offers a chance for kids to "fill in the blanks" as they listen to a presentation (code: lecture) with the proper word that completes their document. In the following example, a science teacher tells the story about plants, and the students are asked fill in the blanks as they listen.

   1. "In the process called _____, plants make their own 'food.' By converting _____ into _____, the plants create and store nourishment that helps them _____."

How did you do, without the lecture? By answering that question, you have just experienced an alternative to guided notes. Instead of jotting down what the teacher said (or the movie narrator or the textbook), you, the learner, have tapped into your own prior knowledge and have made a hypothesis, and you have a record documenting it. Now, as you progress in the learning experience, you can alter your "guesses" with different (and far more meaningful) information.

2. A second alternative to guided notes is for the teacher to give the completed paragraph to the students and ask them to process it personally. Students could do any (or all) of the following:

   a. Identify unfamiliar vocabulary and keep a record of the words in their note-making notebook.

   b. Draw a visual representation of what the reading means.

   c. Write down three questions *not* answered by the paragraph, ones that they may have to explore later.

   d. Rewrite the paragraph in their own words without using the author's words (except technical ones like "photosynthesis").

3. Teachers give notes (and students are asked to take notes) because...

   a. They always have.

   b. Their favorite subject matter college professors did.

   c. Transcribing improves understanding.

None of the offered answers aligns well with students making their own meaning; again, having a record of what the teacher said usually aligns with a testing strategy calling for remembering, not understanding. Note making, in contrast, demands that students think as (or before) they write and record their own ideas for further reflective analysis. Later, they can see their own progress, or at least, their own changes.

So, another variant that captures the intent of note giving and which does borderline justice to note making is the use of an outline; the science teacher provides this outline and students jot down their understandings as the teacher talks. Here is one such outline:

1. How do plants eat?

2. How does photosynthesis happen?

3. What is a plant's "food?"

However, an important step *must be added* if this outlining is to have any positive effect on learning; the teacher must allow feedback on the notes taken/made. This can be done by collecting them and reviewing them, not just for accuracy but for "diagnostic purposes": What did the students think was said? The made notes can also be shared in collaborative groups where students can (a) ask (clarification) questions about things that are different on other people's papers; (b) write a teamed "best answer" for each question; and/or (c) guess about what the teacher thinks is "most important."

Notably, the real cognitive engagement (and deepening understanding) involved in the use of the *outline* comes after the notes are recorded and during the sharing with others or, perhaps, with the rewrite sparked by the teacher review. In the latter case, teachers find themselves reading each student's notes every day, which, of course, no one has ever done. In the sharing scenario, feedback is immediate and valuable.

In conclusion, this extended treatment of note making arises from two salient existing teacher practices. First, teachers want to give notes so that students have a tangible record of important information. By the way, this is why many of us still have kids "copy the notes from the board" (UGH!). There is no thinking necessary in that time-wasting, but common, activity (and there is absolutely *no* research support for its use).

Second, because of historical precedent, note giving "feels" like what should happen in a real secondary class. However, once one grasps the notion that the student must think for herself and that feedback helps her rethink her ideas, the transcription and documentation process fails. Some version of note making, in which students construct and write their own ideas and keep them for further analysis/reflection/modification, is necessary for fully engaging the student who is viewed as a thinker who *matters*.

Grade Wisely

As educators begin to look carefully at the eight ENGAGING factors, they may see that the items 2 through 7 are empirically testable variables—they are strategies that work well. However, large chunks of items 1 (entice effort through relationships and community) and 8 (grade wisely) are far more philosophical in nature. They focus on decisions that teachers make that flow from their senses of fairness, justice, and an understanding of their roles. These items are perhaps less amenable to change than are the other ones.

Thus we come to the issue of grading; it raises its ugly head because it has to, given the way that schools were developed to stratify society and promote competition. (My bias is evident.) Things like grade-point averages, honor rolls, and class rank were not meant to help students (or even to measure achievement) but to stand as rewards, sanctions, and punishments, and to identify winners and force out losers. My initial ideas here are to have you think deeply about grading structures, compare and contrast suggestions, and make sure that you have chosen one that supports your real belief system.

Let's look at several cases of teachers grading teens. What do you think of these? (Better yet, see if you can find someone to talk with about these; you'll be fascinated by the limitless interpretations and suggestions. You may wish to use a T-bar to chart your reactions if working alone.)

- ♦ Ms. Phillips sees grades as motivators. Half of her first quarter grade is built on an individually taken "essay" test score and a group-graded team project. Another 15% is calculated by a daily participation grade. The final 35% is individually negotiated, a contract developed by teacher and student.

- ♦ Ms. Sanders, who sees grades as a form of justice, gives a quiz every Friday (each is worth ten points); the ten quizzes in the quarter are totaled, giving a score out of 100. The students can choose to write a bonus paper worth five points. Combining all of these items gives a quarter grade.

- ♦ Mr. Matthews sees grades as a necessary evil. He gives three 100-point (individual) multiple-guess tests each quarter, plus a team-graded 100-point project and a required individual project worth 100 points. Students choose to drop one of the five scores, the other four are averaged for the quarter grade.

- ♦ Mr. Jordan gives a grade every day of the semester, using a five-point scale. These are built on quizzes, tasks, projects, and discussions that take place during class. At the end of the quarter he totals the points for each student. The top 15% get an A, the next 20% get a B, the next 30% get a C, the next 20% get a D and the bottom 15% get an F. (This was how they did it at State U and he believes that it was fair for him and is fair for his students.)

Each of these four practices is different, legal, and being used, but none is perfect.

Although you may not want me to tell you how you should teach, it may anger you even more if I try to tell you how to grade teens; doing this task is an extremely idiosyncratic enterprise and each of us wants to believe that we are *just* in our decisions. However, I do ask you to consider these factors as you conceptualize your practice for the next year:

♦ Your students themselves may have strong opinions about what makes a grade "fair" and may prosper by talking about these with you and their classmates. There is a good chance that these are different from yours. Trust can be built by this dialogue and any resulting negotiating of meaning will only help class operate.

♦ Giving students "more" chances to improve grades is *not* self-defeating. Treating efforts as drafts or offering bonus points does two (positive) things:

• It suggests that you care enough to honor their attempts at improvement and have paid attention to their work.

• It suggests that you see each of them as an individual, and that treating them "the same" is *not* a way to recognize their equality.

An example may help muddy the water even further.

On a Monday, Jackie gets ten of twenty items correct on her spelling (ugh!) test in English. She studies all that week, takes the same test on Friday and gets all twenty correct.

_____What grade does her teacher record for her on this task?
50% because that is what she got
100% because that is what she got
75% because that is the average of the two tests (although she never scored that mark)

…and since I am trying to be cute (and challenging):

100% because that was her most recent show of understanding
P because it should be a pass/fail item
F because it should be a pass/fail item
50% plus a bonus for effort
a C because the class average on test #2 was twenty.

Of course, the answer is "it depends!" It depends on the belief system and the policy structure of the teacher and its recognition as acceptable by learners. However, perhaps the wisest policy is the one that produces the most ENGAGING effects on teen learners.

Let's continue with one more consideration. The entire process of ENGAGING is built on the premise that teens are thinking, intelligent, and valuable human beings, worthy of *mattering* to us. If so, a grading structure should enhance that philosophy.

- Issues of lateness of work should be dealt with as individual problem situations, ones that the teen should take responsibility for, and ownership of, herself. Extensions, deductions, and so forth should all be mutually negotiated by teacher and student. (Becoming a dropout results from feelings of personal irrelevance and alienation. These same feelings are evident in low achievers who stay until the end but never prosper.)

- "Re-dos," such as Jackie's situation suggests, should recognize real achievements by learners and their attempts at taking responsibility. "Automatic points off" and "averages" are seldom used to assist the students' growth *but* are used to ease the enormous job demands on the teacher. Fair grading policies should also be considered effective motivators, not just rubrics.

- A teacher's grading policy should work to get the most students to try their hardest the most frequently and should lead to a sense of community within the class. Grades should also allow every student a chance to experience success on a regular basis and should hold open the chance for each student to meet his or her expectations and goals on a regular basis. "Grading wisely" really means those teachers must adapt for individual differences far more often than has been done in the past.

Reprise: Elaborating on ENGAGING and Differentiating for Reallygood

Once again, welcome to the world of secondary social studies. This time we are looking at a middle school classroom. As you read, think about Shaneeka's developing situation, Mr. Reallygood's attempts to create active and curious learners, and his use of the Two-Step, as well as his commitment to the ENGAGING process.

A rainy, cold and gray November Wednesday finds Shaneeka, a tall and thin 14-year-old, sitting in her third period eighth grade social studies class in Small City, U.S.A. She is waiting for the bell that will signal the official beginning of class. She chats idly with the boy next to her, Preston, about the project that their teacher, Mr. Reallygood, wants from them at the end of the week. The third member of their team, Wallace, has been out sick all week and no one has seen him in school today. Just as they are about to go up to the door and ask Reallygood about it, the bell rings and he moves to the front of the room.

11:03 "Good morning, guys. Nice job on getting here on time and being ready. Andre, great job on putting up that poster; those newspaper articles are exactly right. Marsha, I got all your homework and, by the way, welcome back to class. Please let's have a nice round of applause for Marsha."

The class claps loudly and several "hoots" ring down as well.

A rising Marsha shouts out: "Thanks. Thanks. It is good to be back. Your card is still on my door at home." Her smile seems genuine and she lightly eases back into her seat.

Reallygood continues: "We have to get to work today, there is much to be done. As you can see on our agenda, the Western Movement team projects are going to be shown on Friday. All the teams are on track, but Preston and Shaneeka, I have to talk to you. Wallace is going to be out until next week so we have to decide how to modify your work. Also, two teams—yes, you guys on Red and Brown—have to rewrite your *blueprint* with the changes you decided on yesterday. All six teams still are in the running for an A on this project and with the quarter ending Friday, this is a good time to keep working. Everybody stop a moment and jot down on your white boards *two* questions that you have before we get to work. You have thirty seconds."

Class members write on boards, except for Franklin, who cannot find a marker, and Otril, who is simply staring into space. Quickly, Reallygood continues: "OK. Now get in your teams, share what you have, and be ready to give me one good one."

It takes a few seconds for the class to rearrange itself in small clusters and Reallygood moves around and positions himself next to Otril. When it is time, he calls on the slouching boy.

Otril looks at his paper, pauses, and then reads, "What if we don't get an adult to sign off on the visual part?"

Reallygood: "Big problem! Good question! You all have reading-study second period Friday. If it isn't done by then, Mrs. Jones, Mr. Chrysler, and Doug from the University will be there and they will do it. But you have to ask them ahead of time. Why don't you write them a note asking them if they'll help? It is only fair to tell them ahead of time."

A few hands jump for the sky. Individual student comments are heard and Reallygood nods at each.

"Do we really have to include the miniplay? What if somebody is out?"

"How come everybody has to write a summary? Can't the leader do that?"

"My computer was down last night. Can I go to the library right now?"

"We can get up to 100 points for a contribution grade. What if we got someone who doesn't work hard?" As that question was finished, the female speaker glared at a young man, Anthony, who is sitting sideways in his chair, appearing exhausted.

"Can we use the pictures in the book *and* the ones we've found from the search?"

Raising his arm, Reallygood smiles, and then responds. "These are all good questions and will help us get going today. First, keep your rubric and the project guidelines handy all day today. We have another hour and will get much done if we stay focused. Second, I ask that everyone work with their partners and urge each partner to try his or her best. Remember, we do want excellence! The more each one of us works and learns, the more each one of us grows. Rick, I'll write a pass for your whole team to go to the Media Center, OK? The other questions will get handled when I come to your work stations. Now, get going."

The 23 students gather in their teams and the buzz of purposeful cognitive exchanges begins.

11:11   Reallygood has moved to his second team of students. While there, he closely studies the paper on Max's desk marked "Outline." Finally, one of the students, Anwar, looks up and asks, "You don't like it…right? We aren't sure what to do about the Plains Indians. They got, well…it wasn't fair."

Reallygood looks at each member of the team and asks, "Should that be a major part of your project? If you agreed, you could make it the centerpiece and the theme." Three students glanced at the fourth, Shaneeka, who is part Native American. They were quiet until she spoke: "If we all think so, well, it is fine with me. I don't know, but I think it would be good for everyone in class to know this stuff." The assent of the others was quiet but obvious.

Reallygood looked at the student, Maxine, who had the role card *leader* in front of her. "I'll need a paragraph about this for my file and all four signatures. OK? You also have to make sure you can be ready for the deadline. This shift may cost you time."

Reallygood then turned to the neighboring group, which seemed to be arguing with itself. "Whoa. What is going on here?"

The largest student, ruddy complexioned Andre, complained loudly, "They always say my ideas are stupid and that they are like bad TV. Well, I checked out the pictures in the text and I like my idea a lot."

Before anyone else can speak, Reallygood cautions them: "You guys should be in the middle of the work by now. You do have to listen to each other, but everyone has to follow the team's decision and be nice about it. OK?"

The students make eye contact with each other and a quiet pause ensues. After a long eleven seconds, they all nod, smile a bit, and go back to work. Reallygood moves their visually built blueprint back to the middle of their desks and reminds them that they had agreed that this was a good plan and that everyone had to be involved. He was stern, but encouraging, as he moved further through the room.

11:33   At this point, Reallygood has taken Mo, a slightly built red-headed girl, out in the hall. His words could not be heard, but he was smiling, gesturing, and nodding his head as the girl went from frown to smile to laugh. After five minutes, she reenters and returns to her team.

Reallygood retreats to his desk, where he reads from clipboards on his desk. Students continue on their tasks and the murmur in the room remains as it had been for the past few minutes. He then changes the large sign on the wall in the front of the room. It reads "Word Wall for Western Movement." Six of the words were in *red* while the other twelve were in black. "Hey guys…" He stopped the whole class, interrupting their work intentionally, saying, "Don't forget that your skits and music *must* include the six red words that we always cycle through every unit and you must use at least six of the other ones. I have to make sure that everyone of you can think with each of these concepts. I didn't see them on every one of your organizers."

He returns to his desk, signaling that the students should get back to work, which they did, except for one group. He walks over to them and calmly says, "Get going. I'll stay here to see that you can make progress." He waits three minutes, watching.

11:55   Calling the class back to its original form, Reallygood has every student take out a sheet of paper and number it from one to six. "Pop quiz!" This is a signal that he wants to find out what each of them is thinking, while giving them a chance to reflect on their cognitive contributions from that day. "You know the drill. Each item gives you sixty seconds and you can collaborate with the friends around you if you want. You have to stay in your seat and chat quietly. At the end of the quiz, you can use the last three minutes of class to add anything you want and clean up any confusions you have. Ready…?"

Reallygood then uses this process to have students respond to these six items:

1. Who on your team has the most difficult part of the project and why?

2. Why are we studying the Western Movement, anyway?

3. How should we talk about the Western Movement: Is it "brave settlers headed West" or "Native people being invaded?" And why?

4. What part of this chapter would be interesting to your *other person*? Why? (Note: early in the year, each student designated someone outside of class as his or her *other* and at various times, she or he must chat with the *other* about class content or proceedings.)

5. Please briefly sketch what part of your team's skit will look like.

6. How was today's class work session either like *or* unlike being a salesperson in a store?

As each item is introduced, the class responds with a murmur and an occasional clarification, but they don't delay because the clock is running. Some students work totally alone, others choose to chat with those close to them. When the six minutes ended, Reallygood claps his hands, says thanks, and tells them to either give him the paper now or on the way out. He also reminds them to keep working on their part of the project, to have a good day, and to make sure that their workplaces *are* ready and clean for the next person.

A bell signals end of class. The students leave the room in an upbeat and friendly manner, many of them wishing Reallygood well. He stands by the door, chatting as each leaves the room: Shaneeka is last and says thanks and smiles as she leaves.

As you reread and reflect on this passage, answer the following questions:

1. What strategies did Reallygood use to build a sense of community and to motivate each student to do his or her best work?

2. How is his instruction designed so that each student will develop a deep and (personally) meaningful understanding of the desired content?

3. How did this teacher try to use student–student collaboration?

4. What is the evidence that this plan seeks to use active and integrative learning procedures and active and complex assessments?

5. How were graphic organizers used to help students structure their understanding?

6. What is the evidence that this teacher uses powerful interventions, including ones that differentiate by (multiple) intelligences?

7. There are expectations that students will document and record ideas and information. What evidence suggests that these (conceptual) notes will be made by them individually rather than simply replicated by them?

8. Grading is a complex issue and one that has great influence on (a) student motivation, (b) student self-perception, (c) eventual life options, (d) classroom atmosphere, (e) teacher expectations, and (f) teacher reputation. What does Reallygood's approach to this part of the job seem to entail?

Author's Comments

I hope that you felt accomplished when you answered the eight questions for yourself. To me, Reallygood is striving to use all eight of the factors and has created a prototype middle-level classroom as well. His students are active and thoughtful; they are using powerful organizing structures and working in different intelligences; they are collaborative and have created community; they keep records of their thinking; and he seems to value and validate them and grade them in a way that keeps them upbeat and persistent. They are unique learning individuals and the teacher has allowed their differences to be used in meaningful ways. (Students will think that he is "fair.") That is pretty good work, and as you will learn in the next chapter, consistent with the scholarship on effective contemporary pedagogy.

3

From Practice to Theory and Back to Practice: Scholarly Support for ENGAGING

Essential Question

Why should I believe that this ENGAGING approach works?

Note: Read this chapter *after* you have read Chapters 1 and 2!

Not every chapter in every nonfiction book needs its own introduction. This one does. Please read this section and consider it to be an explanation for the chapter's content, form, and purpose within this text.

As a long-time educator, I have seen many trends come and go, and I have read widely about trends that perished before my time. Given that truth, there is a contemporary trend that may last a long time. Categorically, I can make the following claim without a shadow of doubt: *Never before in educational*

E	entice effort
N	negotiate meaning
G	group collaboratively
A	active learning
G	graphic organizers
I	intelligence interventions
N	note making
G	grade wisely

history have teachers wanted and needed to know more about research and scholarship than they do now. This trend may be permanent.

No longer are we talking about research as irrelevant, theories as inconsequential, or scholarship as "ivory tower" pontification. Educators are studying theories and theorists and research is being taken seriously. I cannot imagine that this pattern will cease and that we will revert to the "old days" of thoughtless and uninformed practice. Idiosyncratic and "anything goes" teaching practices are fading, being replaced by carefully studied suggestions—research is now a tool to be taken seriously.

I maintain that the use of the ENGAGING process will change people's lives. Teachers will find their work more satisfying, enjoyable, and successful. Teens will find that they and their thoughts matter, and will, in turn, create a greater place in their hearts for more thinking, learning, and knowledge. Parents will be relieved that their children have less angst about schooling (and are now proud of their products.) Employers will appreciate the benefits of a more highly educated workforce and profit from having experienced and willful problem solvers and collaborative colleagues.

But the ENGAGING process is *not* just my opinion, or how I do it, or a bunch of good ideas, or what worked for a teacher I once had. In the past, teaching was mostly built on experienced models (the way I was taught) *and/or* by a form of apprenticeship, copying from others (which many less-informed thinkers still see as a valid way to approach teacher education). Today, we are looking to professional scholarship to ground our practice.

Today, we are fortunate to be realizing the first fruit of what Howard Gardner calls the *cognitive revolution*. After 100 years of simplistic behaviorist (stimulus–response) psychology, we now have scholars who are studying human minds as they learn, we have technology that allows us to see the "human brain in action," *and* we have access to a huge mountain of relevant research to plod through as we plan our daily decisions. (The amount of written scholarship coming out each year is staggering.) However, where does a teacher start as the teacher begins to interpret and study this pile of educational writings?

Here is my short answer: with me and this chapter!

Having integrated the ENGAGING process from my own years of reading, thinking, and study, I wish to share my "take" on a few written documents that both support my suggestions and provide me with a forum to entice you to read them on your own. The chapter is not simply a review of the literature nor is it a brief annotated bibliography. It is not a "top ten" list, as we used to know them. It is my sharing with you my ideas about some powerful writings and telling you how they can help your practice.

The chapter has three chunks. First, I offer you a set of regular, old-fashioned *journal articles*, the kinds of things that teachers do read if they read at all on their own. These "think pieces" are comparatively short, written in a persuasive tone, supported by strong scholarship, and pointed toward some useful suggestions. They are easily found if my comments on them whet your appetite for your own reading.

Second, I have tackled a few long narratives (*books*) that touch critically important topics and do so in an exhaustive fashion. Reading this kind of thing takes time, energy, and, preferably, a "reading collaborator" with whom you can chat; these are limited resources in a teacher's life. Hopefully, my interpretations will give you a meaningful awareness of the book's content and offer some valuable suggestions for your work. (And, of course, they do support the ENGAGING process.)

Finally, the third set of articles is tied directly to the research base that is almost always invisible to practitioners. I have chosen a few representative *research studies* to demonstrate how researchers develop their beliefs, theories, and in some cases, studies. There are fewer of these in the chapter because they represent the type of reading teachers seldom do and are unlikely to begin to do on their own. They are pointedly older than the selections in the other two areas: I subtly want to show you that the results of such investigations have been available for a while and that the findings stand the test of time. I want you to trust that more recent research has not refuted the findings and have provided more evidence for my claims. (Determining the validity of this claim was my job before I wrote these words and is the continuous task of future researchers.) Future educators must count on linking the university's world of research with the K–12 world of application and practice better than has ever been done before.

I also wish to mention the last page of the chapter, which offers a minitest to help you assess yourself *and* help you remember and reanalyze some common meanings found in the readings. Try it—it is a low-stakes assessment and you may find it interesting.

Please do not consider this chapter a luxury that can be avoided or a long-winded package to make the book longer. It is *central* to the elaboration of what has been said already. The thinking you do about the supportive scholarship and my suggestions is a process that will assist your attempts at visioning future implementation. You will have a richer and deeper understanding of why I trust the ENGAGING framework, and you will also have a new set of insights into how to maximize its use in your classroom.

The answer to the Essential Question at the beginning of this chapter is as follows: The contents of this chapter provide scholarly support for a belief that the ENGAGING process will help teachers reach and teach every teen.

Ten Journal Articles That
We All Should Know Well

Journal Article 1

Mayer, R. (2004). Should there be a three-strike rule against pure discovery learning? The case for guided methods of instruction, *American Psychologist, 59*(1), 14–20.

Mayer, a long-time contributor to the enormous pile of research on human learning, felt compelled to write this brief and well-argued piece *against* "discovery learning." Constructivist strategies are often perceived as calls for a laissez-faire approach to teen learning: "let students choose something they like and go off and study it." This is a caricature used against the theories/practices of many scholars and educators (and could be used to argue against many aspects of the ENGAGING process). However, this "review of the research" by Mayer destroys the myth of the value of unguided discovery and clearly supports the type of interventions and scaffolding offered by thoughtful use of the ENGAGING process.

Citing others, Mayer says that guided discovery works very well when two conditions are met: (a) prior knowledge is involved in sense making of new information and (b) integration of the new information is recognized and integrated into an appropriate knowledge base. These notions suggest that teens can understand what they have thought about and can articulate to others. Moreover, these conditions are exacerbated when students are challenged to negotiate meaning for themselves, rather than memorize "right" generalizations and theorems, *and* use active learning and active assessment as opportunities for knowledge construction under the keen eye of a teacher.

Interestingly, Mayer's second point calls for both metacognitive awareness and reflection on the part of the students, which *do not* regularly occur in the cases of a traditional dissemination approach *or* in a pure discovery approach. Whereas the former attempts to ignore prior understandings and schema, the latter do not force students to clarify what it is that they've "discovered." In a structured classroom in which teachers use exploration of students' prior ideas and experiences, the use of strategies that help learners organize their investigations and that demand that students explain their "final and new" understandings will result in a great deal of conceptual gain. Use of the ENGAGING process, of course, promotes those ends, and is often perceived as a joyful and fulfilling enterprise as well.

Stating that a teen "takes ownership" of learning does *not* mean that standards are ignored, important content is ignored, or that he or she is left to work without help.

Teachers should provide multiple learning opportunities, help set the content in an appropriate and meaningful context, provoke challenging levels of dissonance, and, by all means, be available to help the youngster broker the learning experience—to thoughtfully recognize what she or he has ultimately learned or "discovered."

Journal Article 2

Muir, M. (2001, November). What engages underachieving Middle School students in learning? *Middle School Journal*, 37–43.

In a theory-building piece, Muir has painstakingly analyzed the musings of six actual Middle School students regarding their views about "what works in school." This is a fascinating read that offers us some ideas about how these youngsters, the self-proclaimed underachievers, view our efforts to make school meaningful for them. Muir integrates these observations and insights to develop a model of "meaningful engaged learning," a model that is very closely aligned to mine.

To Muir, there are four key factors that need to be recognized as teachers contemplate the learning expectations within their various units of study.

1. *Environment:* Glasser's four motivators—fun, freedom, sense of belonging, and power—stand out in the students' words. They want to be interested in their work, they want to enjoy themselves, and they need to be (emotionally) safe in their efforts. A teacher must ask "What is the status of the environmental reality ?"

2. *Experience:* The need for active learning predominates in their words. (Although the students respect a place for what they call "book learning," that place seems to be distinct from the central thrust of inquiry. They tend to see textbooks as supplements and resources, not as a reservoir of knowledge.) Differentiation and diversified "study" are basic to their hopes for a good education. A teacher must ask, "What do I envision each teenager doing in this activity?"

3. *Meaning:* The teens in this study stress that they want to develop knowledge that matters to them, ideas that actually answer real question that they have. They want to think about school material that has salience in their lives, and they want to decide its importance. A teacher must ask, "Why would they want to think about this content ?"

4. *Motivation:* In a very interesting way, these students say that they want to become curious and examine issues that spark their curiosity. In Middle Level parlance, this can be seen as

linked to the "integrative curriculum" that begins with the students' interests. A teacher must ask, "What is powerfully interesting in the investigation of this topic?"

Digging a little more deeply into Muir's four-part model, one finds that he has really built it on the foundation of nine essential elements (a term that will make Middle School people in New York smile). In the following paragraphs, I offer my interpretation of his nine elements as pieces of advice to teachers who are planning to utilize ENGAGING.

- ◆ Environment
  - Build positive relationships with every teen at every available moment, creating an environment of caring, support, and encouragement. (Students might not mind being "corrected" or "reprimanded" *if* [a big *if*] they feel that their relationship has been strengthened by its resolution.)
  - Offer help as students work and create conditions that utilize peer support as often as possible. (Students need to feel acceptance and respect from their peers.)
- ◆ Experience and Motivation
  - Assign hands-on and minds-on activities that
  - Tap into their differentiated abilities and
  - Appeal to their diverse interests.
  - Do not bribe them, using "stars and awards," but do
  - Offer choices that are real, valid, and appealing.
- ◆ Meaning
  - Use the upper levels of Bloom to guide your authentic assessments, so that students are creating, deciding, or analyzing and doing real (meaningful) thinking and developing deep understanding.
  - Always have students reflect so that they can link their school learning to aspects of the real world, including the social and emotional insights they gain in their projects.

Other connections to the ENGAGING framework are plausible and noteworthy, but three key notions leap to the front as I compare and contrast Muir's approach with mine:

1. Students are not lazy but are very selective as to what they'll devote their energies and efforts into doing. School work (especially a project) can be attempted, but it has to "feel" like it is a meaningful and interesting thing to do. They have to be able to develop a real and acceptable answer to the question, "Why should I do this?"

2. Students need to feel important in their work. Classroom community has to be a safe and supportive reality, and the individuals must be valued as individuals. It sounds preachy to keep hammering at this point throughout the book, but we cannot underestimate the importance of this simple truth. Frankly, many teenagers *are not* important to many adults, including teachers. This sad reality crushes many intellectual sparks and kills many desires to achieve.

3. Learning is what happens during the teen's active engagement with ideas, *not* as an outcome afterwards—it is *not* purely a result of completion. Process matters greatly: To simplify this point, teens learn only what they think about.

There are corollaries to this point that are worth reflecting on.

a. Class is *not* to disseminate information, it is to engage thinking about ideas.

b. Assignments are *not* designed solely to practice volatile understandings; they are to help teens elaborate on and examine interesting phenomena.

c. Finally, peers are *not* to be avoided or ignored, but are potentially engaging collaborators and sharers of ideas.

Muir has offered us a glimpse into the hoped-for-worlds of underachieving Middle Level learners and, in doing so, has validated much of what the ENGAGING process professes.

Journal Article 3

Tomlinson, C.A., and Kalbfleisch, M.L. (1998, November). Teach me, teach my brain: A call for differentiated classrooms, *Educational Leadership*, 51–55.

This article precedes by eight years the Tomlinson and McTighe book reviewed in another section of this text. This was written just when Tomlinson was putting together her thinking about reaching all kids on similar content/topics by different means. Of course, "differentiation" today is an accepted and desired practice, one that defies standardization while demanding excellence and thoughtful achievement by all.

Given that they were writing almost a decade ago, this piece is devastating to the various versions of the one-size-fits-all approach to secondary education. By presenting a lesson from the viewpoint of a conscientious, thoughtful, and high-achieving learner who failed miserably at a well-designed "presentation," Tomlinson's personal experience as a dazed and confused student serves as a reminder about our charges. By ignoring her persona and her understanding needs, the instructor failed Tomlinson, so she failed the lesson; the impetus to adjust instruction was lost and so was the student.

Please note that Tomlinson is not talking in this piece about affective concerns, the sort of warm fuzzies that many secondary teachers (mistakenly) scoff at. The truth is that differential human needs do exist and they make cognitive learning for each student a real challenge. The authors suggest that brain research and the wisdom of practice have provided suggestions for us to consider. They identify three clear findings from this knowledge base and suggest we pay close attention:

1. The learning environment must feel emotionally safe for learning to take place. Affect matters! Again, note that this is a cognitive finding! Intimidation, sarcasm, alienation, withdrawal, and defensiveness, each a response to an unsafe environment, *blocks* any chance for deep thinking and thoughtful applied conceptualization. If one is busy protecting oneself, there is little energy or time left for thinking.

2. A student's brain should neither be challenged beyond capacity *nor* be offered "way-too-easy" tasks. There must be a reasonable challenge to an individual's current thinking. These may take the form of a paradox to resolve, disequilibrium to rectify, a curious insight that needs amplification, or an unfamiliar interpretation that is troubling. Resembling Vygotsky's zone of proximal development, these authors call for appropriate levels of challenge. The learning tasks of an effective teacher must stimulate thinking, build from an individual student's existing knowledge base, and "take the learner to a new place" that is meaningful and personal. In their words, "a moderately challenged learner produces neurotransmitters that facilitate (not impede) learning. If there is only one challenge offered to an entire class, the diversity of that class *assures* that many (or most) are *not* being challenged appropriately. Differentiation, linked to choice, allows a wide variety of challenges to coexist. Moreover, a single task, say a project, or a paper, can be differentially structured to allow every student to work from his or her strength. The key here is authentic assessment used to demonstrate understanding and the avoidance of any form of nonauthentic, single-right-answer tests.

3. Finally, she says that "each brain must make its own meaning." This is akin to what has been called "negotiating meaning" or expecting each student to describe his or her learning in his or her own way. As their brains are different, their prior experi-

ences are different, their senses are different, and their interpretations of stimuli are different, so the end products they create
through instruction should be different, and these differentiated products should be respected by their teachers. (It is important to reiterate that people who give the same response to a
multiple-choice item often do so for different reasons that
never are recognized or identified.)

Note that implied in number 3 above is the notion that we should be
teaching big ideas, concepts if you will, and not testing for factoids and limited information. Certainly, cognitive growth means a reordering and re-
structuring of one's schemata (a changed mind!) *not* simply the addition of a
few facts.

Let me be obnoxious on this one for a moment. Please try to memorize
this right now: pjv@niagara.edu. If you can look away and state it, you've
"learned" it. If you mastered it, give yourself a +1, a candy, or a piece of
praise. But, truthfully, no one can claim that you are smarter than you were
before. You have added my e-mail address to your memory bank (and for
most of us, for just a brief period) but you haven't really gained much. If you
wanted to e-mail me, you could've found it elsewhere in the book or on the
Niagara University website. If you didn't want to e-mail me, your memoriza-
tion is just like that of a millennium of students' other memorizations in
school— you did it for the test, it had no meaning, and it will be permanently
lost soon.

Tomlinson and Kalbfleisch close the article with a list of fourteen characteristics embedded in their *vision* of a differentiated classroom, one in which
differences are respected, turned into strengths, and which allow for a differentiated excellence. Each of these characteristics aligns well with my eight
ENGAGING factors, so be assured that you are "differentiating" when you
follow the ENGAGING approach. You can quote me on that one (and send
me an e-mail to inform me).

Journal Article 4

Wolk, S. (2003, September). Hearts and minds. *Educational Leadership*, 14–18.

In a powerful, short, and clearly articulated article, Wolk tells teachers to
think of their students as real people and to care about them. They matter because they are human beings. In a simple, profound way, he offers several
suggestions to teachers to help them make their classes *real*, that is, a truly engaging experience between people with emotions, feelings, and dreams.

One cannot read this piece without realizing that students really do matter to him—their thoughts and their emotions are at the heart of the school experience as he sees it. He suggests that the relationships among and between

the people in the classroom are the necessary context for any substantial intellectual growth that will stand the test of time.

Specifically, Wolk suggests that teachers utilize the types of personalized and active strategies listed below.

- Use discussion and debate, so that learners see that teachers genuinely care about their insights, ideas, and interpretations. Community, to Wolk, is not just a place, but an active way to live—he sees "community" as a feeling that supports excellence and that trusts thinking. He urges us to "do" community with teens.

- Require students to create interpretive (symbolic) representations of their understandings, ones that are unique and personalized. This multiple-intelligence-based idea results in students realizing that their educations are their own and that they learn what they do (to paraphrase an old Dewey maxim). It also strengthens respect and understanding for diversities that are crucial to developing teens.

- Have students develop biographies as centers of intellectual work. It is difficult for his (Middle School) students to *not* be interested in themselves! By connecting content to their personal experiences, students again make their own understanding explicit. He extends this approach to connect it with Ladson-Billings' (1994) culturally relevant teaching—it validates the experiences that students *bring* into classrooms and recognizes that they have valid and valuable lives. (In other words, their lives do *matter*!)

Finally, it must be mentioned that Wolk, coming from the Glasser tradition, also values fun, freedom, sense of belonging, and power as the motivators that drive youngsters to seek academic excellence. Interestingly, he, like others, cautions against *fun* as a potential trap that is easily bargained away in exchange for academics. Instead, he offers a laundry list of factors that we should keep in mind as we struggle to build the vision of our ideal classroom: "Classrooms and curriculums must be *interesting, intellectual, critical, creative, purposeful, communal,* and *highly relevant.*"

If these seven italicized adjectives exist in a learning experience, they will be felt as "fun" by teens, who will learn a lot. While some of us agonize that our teens spend too much time and too much energy in "fun-related" enterprises, the truth is that schools have never been seen as sources of great joy and curiosity. Goodlad (1984), in his massive study, *A Place Called School,* saw classrooms as boring, intellectually smothering, and vapid. By accepting that one must get to a teen's cognitive change through the teen's affective filter, we may realize that thinking and feeling can be used to help teens take charge of their own growth.

Fun, choice, belongingness, and competence are factors that embrace the heart and engage the mind. Strong relationships and sense of community, the twin pillars of social and emotional support of a great classroom, lead to maximum engagement and high achievement.

Journal Article 5

Willingham, D. T. (2006, AFT). The usefulness of *brief* instruction in reading comprehension strategies. *American Educator*, 39–45, 50.

Please be patient with me in this review. I am going to digress from the prototypical review style that I have been using with other publications in this book and with Willingham's piece, try to ENGAGE you differently.

Read these sentences carefully:

1. My son, Matt, is a very fine middle school teacher.

2. His last unit, on the Western Movement, included a student team-produced skit.

3. Matt's students also selected an immigrant profile and wrote "letters home" about their harrowing experiences in the caldron of the twentieth-century U.S.A.

4. Middle school students in New York State take a comprehensive statewide test in May.

5. Mr. Vermette tries to ENGAGE his learners using multiple tactics, including his own style of questioning, his frequent incorporation of choice, his funny and personalized stories, and his use of authentic tasks.

6. Matt Vermette, who has an infectious smile, is 6' 4" tall, 260 pounds, and a superb athlete.

7. Matt has a master's degree in special education and does a superb job with the "hardest-to-teach" teens.

8. Matt keeps a special eye on the students who do not offer their ideas willingly.

Think about what you read (do feel free to go back and reread sections) and briefly write the central message of the reading. After writing the central message, give the reading a title. Now, answer these eight statements true or false (as best you can), *without* doing any more rereading.

_____ 1. The author's son is younger than the author is.

_____	2.	New York has a middle school social studies exam.
_____	3.	Matt's students do authentic assessments.
_____	4.	The students in this class like cooperative learning and use multiple intelligences.
_____	5.	Matt believes that there is merit in a literacy strategy built on "writing to learn."
_____	6.	Matt Vermette tries to ENGAGE his learners.
_____	7.	Vermette follows a fairly traditional curriculum-content flow in his course.
_____	8.	New York State trusts its standardized testing program.

Now, take a minute and peruse the passage and make any desired changes in your responses.

Finished? Ready? If so, please go on, continue your reading and try to make sense of the messages that I will now try to send to you.

Chances are that during the last few minutes, several things occurred inside your mind as you read and thought deeply. As you read my predictions about your thinking, reflect on their accuracy in your particular case.

> *Note:* if you were not thoughtful and intentional and willful—in other words, ENGAGED—during the reading work, you cannot possibly have maximized your understanding *and* you are less ready to take that prior experience (i.e., prior knowledge) *into* these next comments by the author. ENGAGING the learners/readers "fully" means having them strive to understand independently of your actual presence and demands, eventually internalizing the ownership of their commitment to understand and push themselves. How clear is this? How hard did you have to think/work to make meaning of my words? How hard were you willing to try?

Here are my seven predictions about your "thinking during reading."

1. You turned eight disparate sentences into a holistic pattern, one with a storyline and its own flow. (Note that I didn't use the word "passage" until after you finished the first reading: you probably connected them all unconsciously, but willfully.) If you know Matt, you had little trouble visualizing him in this passage and you had a powerful existing schema to attach the new ideas. If you don't know him, you might have conjured up an image of him in a classroom full of eighth graders and tried

to connect his work with your own understanding of that reality.

2. You recognized that the word ENGAGING was not related solely to its typical commonplace usage, but was directly connected to everything that you have read in this text up to this point. (I pray that you recognized ENGAGING from this book's own title.)

3. You didn't stumble over any of the vocabulary, as more novice readers would have. Therefore, your reading was linear, familiar, and clear. Moreover, you may have thought deeply about the meaning of the word "traditional" in question 7, trying to determine how the test writer used the concept.

4. This next item is a very important point: please think carefully as you read the it! You didn't remember any single sentence that you read per se, but the major conceptual points were easily *grasped*. Long ago, researchers convinced us that learners don't encode exact chunks of knowledge but make meaning that forms a representative and idiosyncratic schema that gets placed in memory. For example: without looking back, answer *yes* or *no* as to whether these **exact** sentences were amongst the eight you read:

_____ a. Matt Vermette is a Social Studies teacher.

_____ b. Eighth graders in New York State take a statewide Social Studies exam.

_____ c. Matt Vermette is 6' 4" tall and 260 pounds and has a great smile.

_____ d. Matt pays special attention to the quiet and introverted students.

…and so on. None of these sentences were shown before, although they may be true in meaning. So, *no* is the actual answer in each case: none are exact replicas. Thus, even though all four are determined to be *yes* or *true* (according to the passage), they were *not* placed into your memory as snapshots or as exact copies, as a tape or video recorder would have captured them. Your brain negotiated their meanings and formed idiosyncratic mental representations, and you remembered them as *true*. This is the process a mind uses during thinking.

Negotiated meaning should be accepted as a human reality and teaching should celebrate this type of differentiated understanding that respects both cultural and individual differences and calls for *non*standardized assessments that require explanations of individual thinking. The days of testing for memorized chunks of information provided a useless type of education and should be relegated to a quaint spot in history's scrap heap.

5. The "grasping" mentioned in point 4 above is related to "inferencing," a critically important skill and one that people who work in service industries and/or professions must have at the ready. Most likely you are very good at doing just that. Solving problems and making decisions, skills highly valued in the workplace, depend on inference making and elaborated thinking. Teaching demands it be done well, done often, and done intentionally.

6. Doing the (a) summarizing (finding the main point) and (b) constructing the title forced you to use some of the "comprehension strategies" that Willingham tells us about in the article. (You will learn about them as you read on.) Moreover, he suggests that it would be interesting to know what comprehension strategies you used during first reading because adults are more likely to use them without prodding than are teens. You may not be aware of your own reading strategies but *to teach them well* you must be able to identify them.

7. Reflecting on how you came to answer the eight true or false items the way you did may tell you a lot about the assumptions that you made as you read, and whether they match those of the writer, something very important on today's high-stakes standardized tests. They may also tell you how you "took the test," fitting your knowledge into the asked item, a task that is fundamentally different than the "free recall" approach called for by the other items.

By the way, the writer of this text (me) answers the eight items this way: The first two are *true*: Of course, no knowledge of the subject at all is required to get that first one correct.[*]

As to the second, it is literally stated that way in the passage.

---

[*] One more note about reading comprehension tests, before we take a look at Willingham's piece in brief detail. One powerful argument for authentic work, and active assessment, is that the assessor has a very good chance of judging ex-

The next six items are also *true*, but demand the use of different types of inferences to get to those meanings. Literally, you were negotiating meaning as you tried to answer them. It is quite possible to have thought well and developed reasonable *false* responses. (I actually hope that you did that because then you'd likely be spending time reexamining the item and the passage, trying to reconcile the disequilibrium that arose. Such a process is often called "thinking" [or, when done with a teacher, "arguing a grade"]. I would have liked to hear your arguments in either case, but the standardized test folks would have scored any *false* response as wrong! Sorry.)

What you have just read should serve as a prior experience that may help you make more useful sense about my comments about Willingham's article. Please recall that after about the third grade most students read to learn, instead of learn to read. This means that a good education demands that they read efficiently, often, for a clear purpose, and reflect upon their interpretations as they transfer them to other contexts.

No secondary teacher in North America today thinks that teens read often enough, well enough, or with purpose or reflectively enough. While this may be hyperbole, there is much truth to this next generalization regarding the reading that teachers expect students to do for their school subjects: By not reading, students limit their cognitive growth and stifle their understandings.

A teen cannot learn enough in a secondary course without reading. Let me say it again, differently: an adolescent's reading matters. The ENGAG-

---

actly what the students are actually learning. But watch what happens when we shift to a badly developed standardized test approach.

Imagine an item like the following on an examination of reading comprehension. In the passage, you read "All xblots gamuc horty tears. No xblots were trunknec." On the test, you're asked; "Do xblots gamuc tears?" And even though you absolutely know nothing about any of these things, you correctly answer *yes*, using the context and sentence structure as cues. This is similar to choosing answer 3 on every item on a multiple-choice test and getting 25% correct (and being treated as if you really did understand that specific 25% of the content).

UGH…again!

The testing game and *No Child Left Behind Act* (NCLB) have created an ugly type of schooling in many places ("Drill and Kill! Teach for the Test! Train for the Test!") and many of us have little faith in what the test results actually say to real teachers about individual teens' real abilities and achievements. When the result of teen thinking is "audible and visible" and exists in a demonstrable product, we tend to believe fully in the assessment process.

Back to the article…

ING process that I am advocating in this text connects to reading in many ways.

I'd like to see students involved with graphic organizers, small group discussions centered on student interpretations, reading for clearly stated purposes, taking their own notes, and *not* being graded for how many details they remember from the assigned pages. I would like to see the word *study* cease to mean *read* (again), and begin to suggest deep reflection and meaning making.

Happily, Willingham has reviewed dozens of studies and concluded that (a) good instruction can increase the comprehension of teens, (b) the use of ENGAGING-like strategies works well to that end, and (c) vocabulary and knowledge growth is linked to active reading and discussion. He uses evidence gathered from the National Reading Panel (481 studies from 1980 to 1998) to call for secondary teachers to teach a few good strategies and have students practice them only a few times (six). But he also reminds teachers to remind students to use these strategies *often:* Once learned, they are never unlearned but teens do forget to use them. (*Note:* Because the majority of teens understand the reading process, they may only need reminders to use the strategies they already know.)

To paraphrase Willingham: The essence of good reading instruction is to convince learners that the point of reading is to make meaning out of the messages being sent in print by writers. This suggests that students must actively monitor their thinking–reading, determining that they either "get it or not." Moreover, by applying strategies such as (a) identifying one's own prior knowledge, (b) using personal elaborations, (c) constructing graphic organizers, and (d) asking and answering one's own questions, students *take ownership* of their own educations.

It is in that taking of ownership that the difference between typical schooling and powerful education lies. Adolescents are far more likely to ENGAGE thoughtfully and willfully think about the content and the concepts of a passage when they themselves are at the center of their own work. When a task or an assignment belongs to the teacher, students will respond with half-hearted, superficial and forgettable efforts; with ownership comes commitment, responsibility, and real gain.

Because much adolescent learning is tied to reading efficiency and frequency, there must be a concern for this process. We are all reading teachers now; Willingham has shown us how to be a good one and offers a promise that it will be worth the effort.

Journal Article 6

Darling-Hammond, L. and, Ifill-Lynch, O. (2006). If they'd only do their work! *Educational Leadership*, 8–13.

People who know me well would anticipate that I'd find a place in this text to honor my hero, Linda Darling-Hammond, who has championed all the right innovations during my lifetime. Her book, *A Right to Learn* (1997), is a classic. In her 1999 article, an open letter to college presidents, she calls a commitment to produce the best teachers possible the main responsibility of higher education. In that piece she cites the factors necessary for student learning, and we have used a key paragraph as our vision statement in the Niagara University secondary program.

The text you are now reading was written for, and to, the grades 5 to 12 teaching cohort of our time. Unfortunately, for us, Linda generally writes for policy makers, legislators, and high-ranking officials. (We are very lucky that she is doing that work in our name!) But this brief piece that she co-authored with Stanford professor Ifill-Lynch provides a common sense interpretation of the ongoing debate over the value of homework, and, by extension, the problem of *grading wisely* when it comes to homework. (*Note:* While this debate rages, Harris Cooper's work suggests that secondary students must spend several hours a week in thoughtful elaboration and/or extension study if they are going to reach the standards that have been set for them. Alfie Kohn, another of my heroes, distrusts most homework as useless and redundant, alienating and impersonal, and a waste of valuable time. This pair of authors offers us a range of opinions worth noting.)

The authors have three intriguing comments, each of which supports the use of the ENGAGING structure. At a time when many adolescents have already quit school or show up only to act like immature children and produce no work of quality, a thoughtful approach to this type of extended engagement with ideas outside of class is warranted.

1. Refusing to do homework creates a power struggle between teachers and students and can easily lead to a breach of trust and community or *crush* efforts to do so. Protecting one's ego by refusing to do an assignment (as opposed to trying and failing) provides a way for alienated teens to take control of their own education—they take ownership of failure! They chose the zero! However, a strong academic culture that values authentic tasks and student meanings of content gives a rationale to work outside of class time. The teen looks at the task and asks, "Is doing this work good for me and is it worth my time?" If the answers are *yes*, the assignments may have value.

I once did a pilot research study that showed me that middle school teens hated and would do almost anything to avoid doing homework, which they saw as work belonging to the teacher. However, they would gleefully try their hands (and persevere) at a project that required them to do some original thinking, tapped their creative juices, and which would be shown to an audience larger than one—they saw that work as belonging to themselves. My advice, built on their case, is simple: Make any assignment an important and interesting original task and not just for the purpose of gaining or losing points.

2. AH! The problem of points! Teachers *cannot* avoid lowering grades of students who don't do their work. Everybody knows that. Truthfully…well…that isn't true. Here are two options to the traditional "docking of points":

   a. If you are giving useless, standardized practice exercises for home, don't count the ones missing; if you have to provide an assignment, give bonuses to those who do this work and recognize their efforts. A third option for required work is the use of an Incomplete, which does not carry the crushing weight of a zero. "Punishment confirms the students' view that they cannot succeed (p. 9)" and does not promote further engagement. This point also reminds me of Glasser's quality school grading concept of using just the grades of A, B, or Incomplete—who wants a C- or a D+? Glasser always insists that if something is worth doing, it is worth doing well.

   b. If the task is meaningful and the students feel some sense of ownership, call it a project, give it a weighted grade, and *provide* opportunities for them to succeed. In the urban schools they know well, the authors note that teachers have provided "study times," offered tutorial-type help, and offered access to physical space for students to work. "Time is expandable" is the rallying cry, so that meaningful work can be respected and completed at a high level of quality—instead of superficial compliance—when students are ready and able to do it.

3. In the name of competence, a hugely important motivator for teens, the authors explain a process by which a "Homework Audit," a type of needs assessment, was conducted and in which students identified truths about their own education—and teachers listened. The notion of a collaborative com-

munity, another basic motivator, comes into play here. The audit was conducted by a team of teachers and showed a schoolwide perspective. It was not a single teacher acting alone. This collaboration confirmed what students were told about the business world's sense of teamwork and showed a committed, unified front of the faculty. Moreover, student organizations also collaborated, helping to tabulate the findings and suggesting changes to accommodate desired and necessary alterations. Students interpreted this as the school responding to their input and began more readily accepting the importance of their "homework." Consider using the audit as a policy intervention in your situation.

I recall being told about a study that suggested that Middle School teens would rather clean their rooms than do traditional math homework. Although I never found the actual citation, the "story" certainly rang true and stuck with me. Every educator should thoughtfully approach the schoolwork issue and develop an approach that gets the students working and grades their processes and products wisely.

Journal Article 7

Scherer, M. (2002). Do students care about learning? A conversation with Mihaly Csikszentmihalyi. *Educational Leadership*, 12–17.

To a certain degree, I am using this brief review to introduce you to the concept of *flow* as discussed by its creator, psychologist Mihaly Csikszentmihalyi. His work has tracked high passion, high involvement, and high-energy commitment to thinking and doing by people of all ages. His research with teens, conducted with an eye for their preparation for the adult worker role, reveals that much of value in school lies in afterschool activities, ones that they have chosen and may have an aptitude for. They invest less energy in their in-class efforts to learn than they do in activities of choice. Let's take a brief look at his piece.

This article offers an interview by an *Educational Leadership* editor with the creator of the concept of *flow*, a concept that describes a state of being that is eerily close to that of being ENGAGED. *Flow* "describes the spontaneous, effortless experience you achieve when you have a close match between a high level of challenge and the skills you need to meet the challenge" (p. 14). It is the state of complete involvement and it represents the epitome of engagement: teens do experience this, but rarely in an academic class or when doing an assignment or schoolwork. It seems to happen more often in sports, extracurricular activities, and at play.

True total engagement would approach a flow experience. If we're careful in our plans and our interactions, *flow* will happen far more often than it does now, and in our classrooms! The author's research with 1,000 teens nationwide shows that students rarely have *flow* in history class, but occasionally do in computer class.

Why in computers but not in history? What is it about computer class that makes mental sparks flow?

Perhaps history/social studies is the ultimate meaningless school experience: studies (Goodlad, 1984; Stodolosky, 1998) show that it is often seen as a simplistic, homogenized, and impersonal set of facts to be memorized by uncaring, unchallenged, and bored teens. Real historians may shudder to hear this, but there may be little thinking expected in the traditional classroom (where a listen-right-now-think-about-it-later mentality reigns). Social studies is supposed to be about producing thoughtful, insightful, and democratic citizens, but classroom preparation for that life task does not seem to match that goal.

Computers, meanwhile, may be the ultimate personalized school experience: The machine does what you want it to do and you have total power over its operation. You and it are both necessary—the computer needs you and you need it. Moreover, vast prior experience allows the students to experiment, play with, and explore their own options with the machine and these conditions optimize the emotional context that allows flow to occur. (Perhaps social studies could be more about "playing with ideas" and less about "mastering the facts".)

Interestingly, Csikszentmihalyi abhors the mass curriculum as we now have it: he sees schooling as much more productive when students have a positive attitude (and interest) in a topic. Obviously, this structure is an impossibility in the K–12 schools and the testing culture we now have. What is not impossible, though, is teaching in a way that recognizes that interests are of central importance to the type of cognitive engagement we seek. Studying for a test in a subject matter or on a topic for which one has no emotional attachment, appears to be a fruitless enterprise. At the very least, (a) working in a collaborative structure and/or (b) conducting some form of independent inquiry and/or (c) personalizing the learning has a chance to produce a flow experience. Flynn, Mesibov, Vermette, and Smith (2004) have the Two-Step model that demands student responses that assure personalization and which generates *flow* more often than other models do.

Finally, in his conversations with teens, the author has seen a pattern between those things they consider *play* and those things seen as *work*. He says that the "best situation seems to be when a students sees a life activity as both work and play." When the student owns the work, it is seen as a valuable and worthy effort; play makes things enjoyable. Thus a classroom activity or an assignment that balances and integrates *work/play* holds the greatest promise of activating flow and producing excellence.

In closing, I ask you to look back at the title: Scherer asks, "Do students care about learning?" Csikszentmihalyi answers with a clear *yes*, but wants to make sure that students realize that they have to work hard to make their own successes. The "extra effort" that produces real success is a direct result of intrinsic motivation; this is the path the student chooses to follow. He wants teachers in secondary schools to help students seek out and embrace the challenging and engaging activities that require a deep investment of self and which "propel them on their way toward becoming productive adults."

Journal Article 8

Schaps, E., and Lewis, C. (1999, November). Perils on an essential journey: Building school community. *Phi Delta Kappan*, 215–218.

As we enter the final few articles of this part of the chapter, I would like to remind the reader of several things:

- I am offering you my "biased" interpretation of what the authors have said and tried to use it as evidence to support my ENGAGING thesis.

- You are most likely a very busy educator, with little time to read widely amongst the mountain of print (and electronic materials) available to you. But if moved, you could easily find any one of the publications that I have written about and compare your "take" on it with mine.

- I have chosen to spread and broaden the range of topics that I have touched on and have not tried to build a monumental case for any one aspect of ENGAGING (with the possible exception being the point that as students think deeply and conceptualize, rather than just try to replicate information, they develop understanding that is long-term in nature).

You could take any one of the ENGAGING factors *and/or* any one of the readings and study it and examine its related literature. As a matter of fact, I urge you to do so: I am confident that you would find the search interesting, full of options and ideas, and a confirmation of my interpretation.

This next piece is about the important topic of *community*. It is stylish today to speak of "learning communities," a group whose members create emotionally safe, socially supportive, and cognitively enriching classroom environments. In such a place, thought is encouraged, questions are sparked, people enjoy each other's company, ideas are generated and examined, and deep conversations happen. Unfortunately, many of us cannot envision such a thing developing in K–12 classrooms, and we trudge on trying to dominate twenty-eight individuals who need to be motivated, managed, and supervised as separate entities.

The folks who want to foster community argue that such a large group structure may be *necessary* for the individual cognitive growth of any one person, as long as the atmosphere of the group is collegial and each member feels safe and supported (Ostermann, 2000). Listen to Schaps' long-time colleagues on the very interesting and successful Child Development Project (CDP) describe community:

> Students experience the school as community when their [individual] needs for belonging, autonomy, and competence are met. Students in such a community feel that they are respected, valued, and cared about…and that they make meaningful contributions.…Students' feelings of (a) acceptance and support, combined with the feeling that (b) they are making important contributions to the group, help to create and maintain feelings of identification with, and commitment to, the goals and values of the group. (Battistitch, Solomon, Kim, Watson, & Schaps, 1995, p. 629)

In other words, to get the most out of learners, the classroom must feel like a good and desired place, in which each person is part of a larger whole. Building positive relationships and fostering community does *entice* maximum effort; it is the greatest motivator available to middle and high school teachers.

This commentary aligns perfectly with the overall tone of the ENGAGING process and is supported by each of the eight factors. For example, negotiated meaning suggests that everyone's interpretation of content is worth thinking about and is worthy of respectful analysis. Individual efforts, such as note making and the use of graphic organizers, lead to a type of diversity that promotes critical thinking and leads to a deeper understanding for diversity itself. Exposure to various intelligences, as they are used as interventions, broadens horizons and offers options.

It is a cyclical process: collaborative constructivism and student engagement foster relationships and a sense of community, which fosters collaborative constructivism and student engagement which fosters…. Once the process is in motion, everyone gains—continuously. ENGAGING practices require and create community. More than anything else, this may be why these eight factors are so powerful. But…

I chose Schaps' article to represent this strand of scholarship because he is a true believer, a researcher in his own right, and has shown the ability to be patient and self-critical with his own findings. In this 1999 piece, he cites "the *perils*" of community building. There are five such warnings and teachers should take heed of them. While the drive to build *community* is in full flight, these cautions are noteworthy:

1. "Caring doesn't mean easy." The term *academic press* is used to capture high-achievement expectations for student learning and the community being built *must* be constructed around high expectations. If social support and encouragement is just good for its own sake, without concern for cognitive change and learning, learning may dissipate. Academic press demands the centrality of cognitive growth.

   We may want to create community so that each teen *learns* and feels safe and supported, in that order. However, the scholarship reveals that the process works in reverse: the student who feels emotionally supported and interested (both increased by a positive sense of community) has an increased likelihood of deep and meaningful cognitive engagement.

   (If I may speak directly to you right now: I cannot get to your thinking processes except through your emotional filters. If you have shutdown your curiosity, dislike my message or style, are under real-life duress, or do not feel supported by others for your efforts, you probably are not reading this for any useful meaning. Reading for meaning making, like any worthwhile thinking, is a willful and intentional process. Controlling your own thinking processes is, by nature, an emotional act.)

   The eight ENGAGING factors were originally drawn from the achievement literature and teacher practice, and are primarily meant to advance the school's academic function. Fortunately, if we build community and press for academic gain, we get both (Elias & Arnold, 2006). Similarly, formal Cooperative Learning was designed to increase achievement and research showed that it did (Vermette, 1998). It did so because it built supportive community that allowed the deep cognitive engagement that was demanded.

2. "Teachers are central in the student-centered class." Like the maestro on his or her Stradivarius, the approach pushed by the eight factors takes a highly skilled, thoughtful, joyful, and dedicated teacher to maximize success for every teen. I am not even remotely suggesting a teacherless classroom, or one where the teacher is a silent invisible "guide on the side," but I am advocating a different conception of teaching (see Darling-Hammond [1999] for a powerful treatise on this point). Students have to do the learning, so they have to do the think-

ing that leads to understanding. Teaching is not just telling, or showing, or assigning, but many other things revolving around helping students scaffold new ideas to their old ones. Good teaching is a masterful process, but it can be learned and improved.

3. "Schoolwide change is essential." It is nice to add that thought as you read alone, right? Well, you can change your ideas and your practice, but everybody benefits more if you make your changes public and if you can bring others into your development. If students experience community in your class *but* not elsewhere in school, the impact is instantly diminished and they get far less experience with the high-yield strategies you employ. In short: try to involve your colleagues in your professional growth.

4. "School values must be examined." Most schools appear to be antidemocratic institutions, with authoritarian power structures and little respect for student thoughtfulness. Certainly, traditional schools were built on factory models designed as assembly lines for efficiency and not to stimulate human development (Armstrong, 2006). Boss management was the reigning style of leadership. If that is *not* an accurate description of your experience, you are in a solid position to seek a sense of classroom community that motivates teens to take ownership and grasp their own growth. If, however, this stilted description of school fits your life, two things may happen when you try to instill belongingness/community and use new instructional techniques:

   a. Surrendering power to students to allow them to fully utilize the sense of community may result in the students abusing you. They may see you as weak, lacking knowledge or confused. (Back in the 1960s, Kozol's Boston kids had to try to teach him how to teach—order people around, give stupid assignments, talk all day about meaningless things, pick on kids—eventually they loved him for his engaging style, began to think critically about their lives, and he got fired.) Patience, confidence and a reminder to them about how they're doing/learning could help this situation profoundly. Many good stories (true ones) have been built around teachers doing things differently—empowering and trusting students—who become loyal advocates once they experience success.

b. Having students take increasing ownership of their own learning (even when they use the techniques and complete the tasks that you mandate) might make you somewhat unpopular with your fellow colleagues. Obviously, this is a reason to *not* "go it alone" (see 2 and 3 above). It is also part of a future wave that expects teachers to grow and change continuously and to use colleagues as sounding boards and sources of ideas. The culture of teaching is changing: we are supposed to thoughtfully try new ideas and not see ourselves as finished products. God knows that we are surrounded by many highly skilled and creative educators who have much to share with us. From this perspective, the eight ENGAGING factors may grow into a much larger number for many of you. At the very least, there are an infinite number of ways to implement each of them and each is a source of a potentially exciting classroom event. (In short, try to involve your colleagues in your professional growth.)

c. By the way, parents, too, may dislike your "new approach" and want you to revert to an educational format that was prevalent in their youth. However, if your school supports your efforts, you treat the students respectfully, you show that you care about them because they "matter" to you (and they mention that fact at home), and academic progress appears to be a reality, they'll love you! Very few parents distrust a teacher who cares deeply about their teen/child and his/her happiness and achievement.

5. The final *peril* that Schaps offers follows this last point about academic growth: "assessment must be aligned philosophically with instruction." Building community and creating student-centered learning activities must be aligned with assessments that call for problem solving, conceptualization, evidence-based decision making, original product creation, and deep understanding, and it probably should be public in nature. ENGAGING factor number four calls for "active learning and active assessment," suggesting that the learning process is as important as the final product. When this approach has been tried, such as was done in Debbie Meier's (1995) portfolio process in Central Park East, everyone was convinced that teens were learning a lot. Of course, they were!

Given that we are still faced with high-stakes standardized-tests and NCLB mandates, teaching for understanding still trumps a traditional practice-for-the-test approach. Interestingly, there is evidence that the best way to prepare for such an examination is to develop the type of understanding of the material that is created by using the eight factors being pitched to you here. The better one thinks, the more engaged the student, the better one understands, and the better the memory and application of conceptual content.

Finally, standardized tests are moving away from the simple, single-answer image they hold in the public's eye; they are moving toward a deeper, richer, and more complex set of challenges. The old test prep, the old meaning of teaching as telling/assigning/memorizing, doesn't have a chance to get the teens ready for that new type of examination (or the reality of adult life).The new test preparation is long-term and thoughtful teaching and learning.

Schap's article may actually be shorter than this review, and for that I apologize. However, his twin issues regarding the importance of building a community of learners and the traps awaiting us as we do are worthy of your careful attention. The work of the CDP should not be lost on us, nor should the evidence drawn from cooperative learning research.

Emotionally secure classroom environments, in a context of academic expectations, foster the deep engagement necessary for each teen to maximize his or her potential.

Journal Article 9

> Perkins, D. (1999, November). The many faces of constructivism. *Educational Leadership, 57*(3), 6–11.

The term *constructivism* is vaguely familiar to almost everybody and a passion-laden, mission-inspiring (either pro or con) word to others. To many of us, the theory of learning encapsulated in this term represents a huge innovation in how educators think about "learning from thinking." It is only in the past few years that educational conversations have begun with the notion of learning, instead of teaching. In effect, the growth of cognitive research has given us a new way of thinking about schooling (a paradigm shift), new findings about the processes involved and a new way to define teaching.

Harvard's Perkins has been a leader in this shift toward constructivism and he uses this short but thoughtful piece to tell teachers about its meaning, its value, and its varied applications in secondary classroom. Combined with his previous work, I see Perkins as one of what he calls here "pragmatic" constructivism's primary advocates. I suspect that he would appreciate and approve of the eight factors of the ENGAGING process.

He does several things in this piece that are worth sharing and your reflection. First, he wants you think about a hypothetical high school student named Betty Fable. She is an *active learner*, learning more from real thinking than from routine exercises. She is a *social learner*, growing cognitively from dialogues with others. Finally, she is a *creative learner*, developing deep understanding from her attempt to demonstrate her meanings via a new and original "product."

Perkins notes that she gains most when she is resolving a new challenge, engaged in deep conversations with others about it, and when she has to synthesize her ideas into a new format. She attends Constructivist High School and is cognitively busy!

Second, he speaks of students mastering different kinds of knowledge, a type of distinction that most teachers never use. His four types are *inert, ritual, conceptually difficult,* and *foreign,* and I suspect that in the future, we won't need them: the six facets will be an adequate instructional focus.

As teachers begin to rely on authentic assessments that incorporate multiple intelligences (Gardner, 2006), the six facets of understanding (Wiggins & McTighe, 2005), choice theory (Glasser, 1986), cooperative learning (Vermette, 1998), the Two-Step (Flynn et al., 2004) and culturally relevant teaching (Ladson-Billings, 1994), these distinctions will make even less difference than they do today. The resulting development of student conceptualizations will be sufficient.

Finally, the opening of his article is worth the time spent finding it online. Trying to be cute while paying homage to Perkins' career, I end my piece with his opening, which he used as an attempt to engage the reader, foreshadow the rest of the piece, and highlight the variability and power of constructivist practices. Most writing is still a one-directional narrative and lacks the power offered by interactive instruction. He clearly tries to produce emotion when he starts his narrative with a *story* about Betty Fables' first day at Constructivist High:

1. In history, she pretends she is a French aristocrat in order to write a letter to an Italian about the French Revolution.

2. In physics, she makes predictions about the weight of objects and their speed in free fall and then her team devises experiments to test their theory.

3. In algebra, she participates in a discussion of the meaning of "simplify."

4. In English, she writes about how a poem by Robert Frost relates to her own life.

At this high school, there are clear expectations for successful higher-order thinking, a clear sense of active learning and assessment, a clear commitment to having students document their own learning, and clear messages about individual effort. I would think that teachers there are also trying to build community, often use graphic organizers, rely on multiple intelligence-based interventions, and grade wisely. If so, this is a perfect example of the ENGAGING process in action.

Journal Article 10

Fredericks, J.A., Blumenfeld, P.C., and Paris, A.H. (2004). School engagement: Potential of the concept, state of the evidence. *Review of Educational Research, 74*(1), 59–109.

When I created the label ENGAGING, I did so for several reasons; it seemed to be what students were actually experiencing when they were deeply involved with a school concept or task. Like the concept of *flow*, it captured the notion of emotionally charged thinking, and it was the word educators used most frequently to represent what they hoped their classes "looked like." I did not intend to turn it into a household word, nor did I wish to brand it as a personal trademark. However, every time you hear that word from now on, I sincerely hope that you think of the eight factors and conjure up the *vision* of effective teaching that this text is trying to help you build. As you know, if teens really *matter*, we will use ENGAGING practice.

With that in mind, I wish to speak to you about this fine article. Fredericks, Blumenfeld, and Paris must have decided that "engagement" was a very important concept and then proceeded to read and review everything that had been written and investigated using that term. Although their thoughts take up fifty pages of the *Review of Educational Research*, several clear findings are worth noting here.

- ♦ The term *engagement* has been used differently by many different writers and thinkers, and generally seems to include three aspects: behavioral, emotional, and cognitive. Thus, being engaged suggests a student's commitment to intentional, thoughtful and joyful effort, the kind expected from use of the ENGAGING factors.

- ♦ No matter how it is defined, it is a *crucial* variable; it leads to desirable outcomes that educators seek from students, including higher achievement and persistence at studies. In other words, ENGAGING works! Their entire article provides widespread support for the specific suggestions offered here, such as moving teens toward taking ownership of their own thinking, toward having a grading policy that keeps student motivation high, toward nurturing relations between and among students and teachers, and toward the use of authentic assessments and choice.

- ♦ The use of the term in the literature is becoming more widespread, both because it has important consequences *and* because it is seen as "malleable": *engagement* can be increased and decreased so that teachers' actions will have enormous influence on teen processes that increase learning. In effect, this confirms the theory of ENGAGING presented in this book.

Moreover, in their closing, the authors mention the importance of "structure;" you surely realize by now that I am not advocating a laissez-faire, free-for-all type of schooling when I urge the use of constructivist strategies and building encouraging and supportive relationships. Teaching is hard work and using ENGAGING is difficult, but will be worth your efforts. Teachers and teaching *matter* too.

Six Books for All Secondary Teachers

Book 1

Bransford, J., Brown, A, and Cocking, R. (2000). *How people learn: Brain, mind, experience and school.* Washington, DC: National Academy Press.

Simply put, this is the most important book published in educational circles in the past decade. I say this for three reasons:

1. NCLB seems to be pushing teachers to "teach" for the test and they appear to have been given carte blanche to do old-fashioned and ineffective "drill and kill" or what McNeil (1986) refers to as "defensive teaching," an uninspired and methodical "going through the motions." Goodlad (1984) describes this routine in a way that is almost embarrassing. *How People Learn* explains the research that supports far more engaging, interactive, challenging, and brain-compatible instruction.

2. Because it is far more about learning than it is about teaching, it is the type of book that teachers rarely read carefully. Moreover, it is not an educational psychology text, with "a million" references to disembodied studies that do not speak to teachers. This is a clear memo written to professionals about what important research says, what it means, and why they should pay attention to it. The content of this text stands as strong evidence for the change from the traditional paradigm, such as the one offered by Hunter (1982), to a constructivist paradigm, such as the one provided in the ENGAGING process.

3. The authors, led by the noted John Bransford, have developed a narrative that does several very positive things for readers. First, as I said already, they write in a clear and friendly man-

ner. Second, they offer brief descriptions of the research studies they deem important, so there is a sense of how a study was done and why it should be trusted. (Many of these reviews are presented in boxed fashion so they stand out from the text and can be easily examined.) Third, this is *not* an encyclopedia of research with every study delivered; the offerings are manageable and appropriate for the topics they consider vital (such as transfer, differences between experts and novices, feedback, prior knowledge, scaffolding, teacher learning, design of environments and [learning for] understanding).

This text also offers dozens of great quotations which could be used as discussion starters (springboards) for teams of teachers, groups of preservice students, or for members of educational groups (such as boards of education) that are trying to understand many of the changes called for by the reform movement. Here is a sampling of my favorites, ones that align well with the ENGAGING process:

- (Quoting Herbert Simon): "The meaning of knowing something has shifted from being able to remember and repeat information to being able to *find* and *use it*." (p. 5)

- "Learners of all ages are more motivated when they can see the usefulness of what they are learning and when they can use that information to do something that has an impact on others." (p. 61)

- "Transfer from school to everyday environments is the ultimate purpose of school-based learning." (p. 78)

- "Transfer is affected by the degree to which people learn with understanding rather than merely memorize facts or follow a fixed set of procedures." (p. 55)

- "Opportunities to work collaboratively in groups can also increase the quality of the feedback available to students." (p. 141)

- "Cognitive changes do *not* result from mere accretion of information, but are due to processes involved in conceptual reorganization." (p. 234)

- "Practice and getting familiar with subject matter takes time.... Most important is how people use their time while learning." (p. 235)

- Finally, there is a quotation from page 141 that I've tweaked slightly so it can be used for many purposes tied to the changes called for in the book you're reading. Here it is: "A challenge of implementing good…practices involves the need to *change* many teachers', parents', and students' models of what effective learning looks like."

What is your model of good teaching? A year before *How People Learn* came out, Darling-Hammond (1999) called for a "redefinition of teaching" in order to increase learning of all students, and Bransford et al. have provided substantial evidence that she was completely correct. Teaching is sparking thinking, engaging interest, and scaffolding cognitive effort. Moreover, in Chapter 1, you observed Mrs. Reallygood teaching science in a manner that is anything but traditional, but one that is certainly aligned with how human brains actually work to develop understanding. In the future, the accepted model of good teaching may be aligned with the vision of the ENGAGING factors at work.

Today, we want all teens to conceptualize, to be able to solve problems, to think critically, to collaborate, and to enjoy and persist in their cognition. In other words, we want them to have sufficient *expertise* to make a better world for themselves. To quote *How People Learn* one last time, "expertise requires well-organized knowledge of concepts, principles, and procedures of inquiry" (p. 239). Teaching for such expertise suggests in-depth approaches with heavy use of student-centered and knowledge-working strategies, such as those offered by the ENGAGING framework.

Book 2

Danforth, S., and Smith, T.J. (2005). *Engaging troubling students: A constructivist approach*. Thousand Oaks, CA: Corwin Press.

Perhaps this is a strange addition to the "book list" that I offer in this chapter, whose purpose is ostensibly to provide evidence for the ENGAGING approach. "Ahhh," you might think, "it is recent, it is constructivist, and it does have the word 'engaging' in the title." You might even be thinking that the authors have exchanged ideas with me. Well, they haven't and they didn't know about the book you're reading while I was writing it, but I hope they read it, like it, recommend it to others, and incorporate some of the ideas into their regular work. We are on the same wavelength and their ideas, and their *stories*, are both intriguing complements and extensions to those found here.

The single most important reason that their text makes this list is that it offers very sound instructional, managerial, and motivational advice to those of us who either teach "troubling" students (those who present problems for themselves and for others in their classes and schools) in regular classes or in special programs. The authors essentially call for active learning, a caring attitude, and a concern that these students have a chance to think, show their cognitive ability in a trusting atmosphere, and not be forced into the traditional school practice of "sit and get," which they cannot handle.

With all due respect to the specialized population that Danforth and Smith advocate for, those last few comments sound like they fit most teenagers today!

I suspect that Danforth and Smith's text will be a well kept secret until educators discover that it has great advice, offers promising suggestions, and that the authors actually recognize the difficulties that "difficult" students present to teachers. The book is a fast read that offers realistic and personal stories that resonate to the "hero" in each of us, and it clearly identifies what it calls its "bias." As you read the next paragraph, a quote from the book, try to keep in mind your current meaning for the eight factors of ENGAGING and my claim that we need to create a passion for thinking and a classroom community that encourages excellent effort and enthusiasm:

> For the many students who resist and oppose the educational structures and activities provided by the school, a constructivist approach means *not only* that we ask the students to open themselves to the knowledge available within the curriculum, but that we make this act of opening up mutual, operating respectfully in two directions....This allows for a negotiation leading to an exchange of ideas...and we engage students in ways that support their emotions *and* thinking, in ways that value their experiences and cultural identities. (p. 7)

Revealing my many biases, I think that Danforth and Smith are suggesting that interactive teaching that demands that students "play" with new ideas (using ideas from their own personal lives) *and* that is done in a respectful fashion will work with the toughest cases in our schools. They suggest that students who have fought the educational system have done so because school doesn't recognize and value their personalities and their individual realities and doesn't attempt to find out what they have to say about "content." To me, this sounds as if heavy doses of the types of suggestions offered in Chapter 2 may stand as motivational and managerial strategies, as well as cognitive processing ideas. If they are right, and troubling students will respond positively to instructional overtures that are challenging, respectful, and personal, we should listen carefully: There is no reason to think that such an approach wouldn't also work with *all* teens. Most importantly, actually listening to their ideas as they examine, interpret, and investigate key ideas—such as is called for by *negotiating* meaning, *active* learning and assessment, and *enticing* effort by building relationships—ought to be powerfully motivating to every student we face.

There are several other very key facets of Danforth and Smith's book that make it both evidence for the ENGAGING process *and* a most valuable read in its own right. First, it concentrates on the use of *stories*. Since Gardner (2005), Carter (1995), and Pink (2004) have made the term *story* respectable, it can now be seen as a powerful and legitimate way to convey ideas. I have used anecdotes and cases as stories in this text, whereas Danforth and Smith use them as a means of offering suggestions, showing strategies, and providing context. Gardner suggests that humans may be "hardwired" to remember information and ideas as stories, and Danforth and Smith take advantage of that theory. They do not offer isolated factoids, research generalizations, or a huge set of theories, but they do offer many anecdotes that help the reader grasp their "point" and understand applications. (Interestingly, teachers rarely speak of the generalizations found in educational research but they nearly always respond to stories and examples that convey those generalizations. I have tried to use that approach in this text, and Pink, writing to business leaders, suggests that success in that realm goes to those who use stories well.)

Second, it recognizes that school learning is social in nature and best develops in a community setting. They are unabashed supporters of cooperative learning, as I am. Their chapter is unrelenting in its rejection of traditional individualized (and competitive) systems, and they tell many good stories about how to use grouping well.

Third, Danforth and Smith's book never backs down from its basic position that teachers must *care* about every single teen, and do so continuously and openly. While the book is making the case that teens who fit its seven categories** of troubling students, the eight themes of caring that it espouses are central to the work of the teacher who attempts to uses the eight factors of ENGAGING as cognitive strategies. Simply put, Danforth and Smith encourage us to make every student *matter*, as professionals entrusted with the re-

---

** Their seven categories of troubling teens are as follows: (1) those who resist and oppose school norms in loud and/or violent ways; (2) those who subvert school norms in sneaky and/or manipulative ways; (3) those who have difficulty making friends and/or sustaining relationships; (4) those who struggle because of depression, anxiety and/or fear; (5) those who have been traumatized by violence; (6) those who feel deeply alienated and/or disengaged from school; and (7) those who are withdrawn and/or isolated from school social circles. Each of these categories is probably easily exemplified by a real teenager that you know from school, family, community, and/or neighborhood. The "stories" that those teens personify serve to make the very case that Danforth and Smith present: These kids really "matter" and deserve the best we can offer strategically and emotionally.

sponsibility to assist them in their total development and as human beings who seek justice, equity, and opportunity for all.

The "eight themes of caring" that Danforth and Smith posit follow. I share them here to entice you to read their words and to remind you how important the affective dimensions of teaching are to teenagers.

1. Teachers must invest *time* with every student, and more with those who need it. This is difficult in the chaotic days that are prevalent in secondary schools, but there is no substitute for the trust and support that time offers.

2. The teacher must always *be there* when he or she is (most) needed. Coupled with the first point, this item trashes the tradition of secondary teacher as "transmitter of the discipline" and as a person who is aloof from the students as people. (Teachers are not the judges of teens, but the advocates *for* teens).

3. Teachers must *talk with and to* every teen as if what the teen had to say really mattered (which, of course, it should). Without conversation and dialogue, there is no way that a teen could picture herself as important to the teacher, and certainly could not believe that her ideas about the content had any value.

4. Teachers must be *sensitive* to the nature of the teen existence. Although many do not suffer from emotional "ups and downs," many do, *and* these carry into classroom dynamics. When the classroom feels like family, when the atmosphere is pro-student and conflict can be resolved without bitterness, everyone benefits.

5. Teachers have to be advocates and *act in the best interests* of each of their students.

6, 7. Caring takes the forms of both *feeling* and *doing,* meaning that it has both emotional and interactive structures. Using Noddings (1992) as their model, Danforth and Smith suggest that teachers think about the kids as individuals *and* act as if the teens matter.

8. The final theme they speak of is one of *reciprocity,* which suggests that classroom interaction is supported by dialogue, negotiation, and respect, and that students are *expected* to give back emotional support to teachers and to other students.

Book 3

Ladson-Billings, G. (1994). *The dreamkeepers: Successful teachers of African-American children.* San Francisco: Jossey-Bass.

Ladson-Billings, G. (1995). But that's just good teaching! The case for culturally relevant pedagogy. *Theory Into Practice*, *34*(3), 159–165.

In this review you get a "two-for" deal—I will be sharing my thoughts about Ladson-Billings' great and critically important book and integrating it with a powerful short article that she published a year later. The latter piece captures most of the flavor, suggestions, and passion that she develops completely in the book, but does so without its size or expense. I require the text in most of the courses I teach at Niagara University because it puts forth a seemingly timeless thesis: American schools fail to teach (low income) African-American students (in this case, California middle schoolers) in a way that maximizes their human potential *and* that this is especially tragic because we know what does work with these kids.

Ladson-Billings wrote this book in 1994, when her study was completed. If you haven't noticed, we haven't changed a great deal since then. (In fact, my morning newspaper cited the pattern that the high school dropout rate in the U.S. was reverting to the awful norms of the late 1950s—the achievement gap lives!)

What is her solution to our failure to educate African-American teens?

Her study carefully tracks the classroom work of eight superteachers, identified by people from the African-American community, over several years. This beautifully designed qualitative research reads well and easy, and it reveals a pattern of instruction that can be seen as constructivist in nature, politically challenging in tone, respectful in practice, demanding in operation and relentlessly student centered. Moreover, its tenets align very well with ENGAGING practice, suggesting universal applications of the eight factors. She calls her approach *culturally relevant teaching* (CRT).

CRT may well be the answer for the inner-city, low income black kids in our schools. Furthermore, most aspects of CRT may well be applicable to all teens, everywhere in Western culture. (In truth, I use a variant of CRT with my students at Niagara University, at least 30% of whom are not American citizens.) Let's examine some of her suggestions, drawn from various chapters:

First, students must experience successes in their schoolwork and these can be made more likely by the use of communities of learners, cooperative learning, building on prior knowledge, respecting every student's ideas and offerings, and treating students' lived experiences as the starting points of investigations.

Moreover, her star teachers were involved with the students and their lives; they connected with the teens beyond their classroom interactions. The teachers made the kids feel that their lives mattered to them. Of course, to these teachers, the kids really did matter! A sense of genuine commitment and strong personal relationships marked the interactions between these people. They shared a common humanity. Ladson-Billings calls this type of teacher the "conductor." The conductor will lead every child to the "promised land" of success *and* takes responsibility for that assignment. The kids will do the learning, but the teacher scaffolds the experience and expects everyone to seek excellence.

Second, in CRT, the teaching metaphor of choice is "mining," rather than "banking." In other words, teachers pull ideas, experiences, and interpretations from students, they do not rely solely on providing ideas and "input' them into minds. Negotiating meaning is the nature of the teaching act—start with student perceptions and have them work through concepts and content that reinforce, challenge, and extend their beliefs and knowledge base.

Given the specific children in her study, this student–teacher (and student–student) interaction always took the form of a socially and racially conscious discussion, which these star teachers did not back away from. They sought to challenge youngsters about the realities that they were living *and* expected the students to make connections between their "local, national, and global" identities. They also truly believed that all students can learn; what is today's worn out cliché was a radical idea in 1994. The point, though, is that they did learn a great deal from those eight teachers.

There is one other aspect of Ladson-Billings' work that is truly more meaningful to our work with teens from underrepresented groups. Although the teaching maxims all align with my conception of ENGAGING, one philosophical point that she makes is not readily apparent in my work. She saw that the great teachers sought "cultural competence" from their charges. Theoretically, one could readily use all eight ENGAGING factors and not see this outcome. Ladson-Billings desperately wants her kids to be "bicultural"; that is, succeed at school learning while maintaining an identity in the traditional cultural identity. Rightfully, she doesn't want black teens to have to choose between their own backgrounds and some ill-defined assimilationist ideal that requires turning their backs on their lived history and culture. They can be black and well-schooled, and the students in her study were both.

Interestingly, all eight teachers in her study were female, although some were *not* black. Apparently, then, white women can teach black students well; however, many readers of her book have asked "where are the male teachers?" There are many plausible answers to this intriguing question, but note that males (white and black) can follow her CRT model, and most likely would experience success in the classroom as the females did. White males (including myself) may have just been slower or more reluctant to change their practice. (Perhaps they will now that they know it works!)

I'll close with one brief quote from the book after I remind you that the topic of multiculturalism and multicultural education has a relatively brief history. When she wrote in 1994, most thinkers were talking about *curriculum* issues of race (and gender). Studying black achievers was seen as the way to close the achievement gap by increasing the interests of minority kids. "They didn't see themselves in the curriculum" was one charge, as was a call for Afrocentric curricular materials. That was all well and good, and a problem, indeed. However, Ladson-Billing insightfully saw the achievement gap and, bluntly, the terrible school achievement record for black Americans as a problem of both instructional practice and content. She says, "but it is the way we teach that profoundly affects the way that students perceive the content of that curriculum" (p. 13).

The way we teach matters and ENGAGING them personally works. To say it simply, if we teach well, all students will be engaged, thinking deeply, and developing meaningful understanding. Because it hasn't happened on a wide scale yet doesn't mean that it cannot happen—instruction trumps curriculum, and always will.

Book 4

Tomlinson, C.A., and McTighe, J. (2006). *Integrating differentiated instruction + understanding by design.* Alexandria, VA: ASCD.

This is an important book at a critical time: Educators have committed to teaching every student (to a historically high set of standards) and have redefined their vision of an educated person. Unlike several generations ago, being able to sign one's name and decode simple texts is *not* enough to call a person "educated." Contemporary education is expected to prepare thoughtful and analytical people for a global and technological job market and for a complex citizenship. There are no clear models as to how to accomplish this, thus providing the rationale for my ENGAGING approach and for the reading of my text.

The authors make a strong case for two pillars of the reform process: differentiating instruction to meet diverse needs of teens *and* teaching for understanding, a process inherently different from teaching to pass (lower level) multiple-choice tests or remember simplified content. The challenge of teaching all to think well should move us all to "play" with the ideas that hold the promise of engaging teen interest and cognition.

In effect, the text asks the *essential question,* "How can I modify instruction so every student develops appropriate and meaningful understanding of important content?" Following are some of the plausible answers Tomlinson and McTighe offer.

First, the concept of the *essential question* must be recognized for what it is—the single most important curriculum idea of our time. At a point where places like California list more than 1,000 objectives for social studies alone and the debate rages over the "cultural appropriateness" of SAT items, the idea that there are *big*, key, permanent, and critically important questions for teens to answer is very appealing. What if we settled on a small number of truly important thematic issues? We'd kill the irrelevant trivial pursuit of thousands of "forgettable" factoids and be able to have students focus their cognitive growth on stuff that matters.

If I may—We treat teens as if they matter *when* we teach them to think about ideas that really do matter!

School has too often been reduced to the presenting of information, usually lists of things like the following:

♦ Letters in sequenced order to spell words that will never be used again;

♦ Steps to solve quadratic equations or to multiply fractions without grasping the purpose of the process *or* the meaning of the answer;

♦ Endings for verbs *not* used in real human conversation in English or Spanish; and

♦ Sequence of events in a novel's plot, a revolution, or in setting up a new franchise.

These types of factoids are easily converted to multiple-guess tests, decontextualized bits of datum that may help during a game of *Jeopardy!* (or *Trivial Pursuit*), or in trying to impress future spouses, but relatively useless in solving problems, creating new interpretations, or making an evidence-based decision. (Note that these are perhaps the most important three reasons for school to exist.)

Here is a test:

_____ 1. The capital of Florida is….

a. Port St. Lucie

b. Tampa

c. Tallahassee

d. Orlando

e. Miami

_____ 2. $(x^2 - 3) \times (x + 1)$ results in….

a. $4x^2 - 3x$

b. $x^5 - 5x^3 + x^2 + 6x + 3$

c. $x^3 + x^2 - 3x - 3$

d. $x^5 - 2x^2 + 3$

e. $x^4 - 2x^3 + 2x^2 + 6x - 3$

_____ 3. Which happened first in The Tragedy of Romeo and Juliet?

a. The death of Juliet

b. Romeo's plea of love

c. The feud between the families

d. The interference of the friend in the relationship

e. The "wherefore art thou" speech

_____ 4. Here are some organs used in food digestion in a chicken: (a) anus, (b) crop, (c) gizzard, (d) intestine. Which is the correct sequence for digestion?

a. a b c d

b. d c b a

c. b c d a

d. c a b d

e. b d c a

Here is another "version" of the "same" four-item test:

1. How do people decide what city should be the capital of a state and why is that an important decision?

2. Show two ways to multiply "expressions with unknowns" and tell why it is important to be able to do so.

3. How could the conflict like the one in *Romeo and Juliet* have been resolved *without* resorting to violence?

4. Compare and contrast human digestion with that of another animal.

The first test gives answers to items in a way that allows the teacher to *assume* depth of understanding—the specific items are thought to be representative of a larger information pool held by an individual. This assumption is, of course, often *wrong*. (Twenty percent of the time one can guess the "right" answer without *any* information pool.) The second test, which forces a far more public performance of "thinking with knowledge," is also more authentic—it asks learners to show what they understand and can be used to show deeper levels of understanding. Furthermore, this demonstration of understanding cannot be "faked," like it can be on the first test.

McTighe (earlier with Wiggins, 2005) makes us realize that educators *want* deep understanding and that it is acceptable to recognize the need for authentic assessment, contrary to the simplistic structures of NCLB. He also says that if teachers do their planning using a system called "backward planning"—from the assessment vehicle "back" to the learning activities—we are more likely to succeed at acceptable levels with all students. If teens knew the very question they were trying to answer, they'd be more likely to do so *and* see its importance more frequently.

Wiggins and McTighe have also suggested that the authentic performance of understanding be tied directly to the essential question, so that grades (used judiciously) do *not* present a totality of little meaningless scores but are indicators of cognitive growth on an important (and negotiated) meaning. (In our examples, your "Test One" score is created by adding the number you got "right" when comparing your responses to an answer key; your "Test Two" score takes into account more of what you actually know about the topics and is more representative of your real cognitive understandings.)

Another example may help you grasp the subtleties of their thinking. McTighe uses a unit on "nutrition" by hypothetical teacher Bob James as a standard example. The unit contains several essential questions that really do matter to teens (including, "Why does it matter what we eat?"). By incorporating what they call the Six Facets of Understanding, they offer multiple and differentiated avenues for an individual to show depth of understanding, none of them tied to a guessing game. I love this "deconstruction" of the concept of *understanding* into six indicators, each demanding different types of student thinking *about* an issue or question.

Here are the six facets turned into questions and applied to the nutrition unit:

1. Can you explain the principles of nutrition and give examples? (*explain*)

2. Can you use anecdotes or stories to show the meaning of good nutrition? (*interpret*)

3. Can you apply the principles in diverse situations? (*apply*)

4. Can you describe how the issue of nutrition connects to other parts of U.S. life, such as poverty, friendships, advertising, and family traditions? (*perspective*)

5. Can you tell how and why other people will react to your thoughts about nutrition? (*empathy*)

6. Can you describe how you thought in a way that helped you learn this topic and tell what questions might still remain for you? (*self-knowledge*)

The Six Facets of Understanding help us conceptualize the term *nutrition* as composed of different attributes and therefore is realistically complex. Different students will have different—and more supportable—replies to the six questions here, all the while showing some understanding of nutrition. Moreover, "nutrition" can be spiraled through the curriculum, allowing for deeper and deeper meaning and better and better student responses. (This is, of course, how real human learning builds on prior knowledge and cognitive engagement; your own understanding of nutrition is much more powerful today than it was when you got some answers correct on a middle school quiz a while ago.)

To accomplish the end of reexamination of ideas and thoughtful development, Tomlinson offers many ideas about student work to make it appropriate and within reach. She offers a series of suggestions, each with an eye for making the individual more self-reliant and willing to take ownership of his/her understanding. In her view, school is not about learning the teacher's material but conducting investigations that help individuals make their own understanding. (Of course, this links directly to the Understanding by Design process.) She posits that when students are helped to see their own strengths and weaknesses and see the importance of learning, they will become responsible for developing themselves: their education is their education and it should *matter* to them! The final step is to develop structures that allow for these strengths to be used.

Specifically, Tomlinson calls for the (a) thoughtful use of preassessment tools (so teachers can work from prior knowledge bases), (b) creation of a safe (affective) environment (so a sense of respect and community can be maintained), and (c) the expectation of a public performance of understanding (so students will know what success looks like).

To use their own words, a chart on page 140 calls for teachers to

> adjust instruction to address…student readiness, interest, and learning profile, including small group instruction, time variance for learning, exploring and expressing learning in a variety of modes, tasks at different degrees of difficulty, and varied teacher presentation approaches.

These two innovations blend perfectly as a backdrop of support for the eight ENGAGING factors and the desire to use those strategies in a humane and caring classroom.

Focusing on essential questions, differentiated ways to "investigate" them, and recognizing different types and depths of responses creates a developmentally appropriate and student-centered secondary approach to teaching. Using the ENGAGING process does all of this, and more.

Book 5

Armstrong, T. (2006). *The best schools: How human development research should inform educational practice.* Alexandria, VA: ASCD.

If you're ever going to read another book about education (after the one in your hands right now), this is my recommendation. Armstrong's book is the "right book" to read next, but *not* because

- ♦ he has a secret formula for classroom success;
- ♦ he has assembled a flawless and indisputable argument;
- ♦ he has incorporated all the right research;
- ♦ he has supported the ENGAGING process (although he does like engaged learning, p. 124).

Nope, those are not the reasons. It is the right book because his argument coherently meanders in support of the case that the reason we really want to have formal education does not start and end with test scores or national economic competitiveness but because we are striving to produce happy, productive, hardworking, socially competent, problem-solving citizens who will foster and promote the ends of justice in a democratic and diverse society.

Although a mouthful, that statement says a lot and means a lot. Here is the reason why: The best of our educational philosophers and scholars have used those kinds of things as the desired outcomes of good education. When, for example, we examine the writings and policies of educational giants like Vygotsky, Dewey, Piaget, Bruner, Gardner, Montessori, and Erikson, we see a benign and caring educational practice that fosters each person's individual gifts, talents, and dreams, and which is appropriate developmentally and culturally.

However, what he calls Human Development Discourse (or paradigm) has been displaced in the United States by Academic Achievement Discourse (or paradigm) and current educational debate is all about test scores on standardized tests and *not* about producing citizens who feel fulfilled, competent, proud, unified, and secure in themselves. To Armstrong (and others I hope), that is a great shame. Having written beautifully about how teachers can best use Gardner's (2002) multiple intelligences theory, Armstrong turned his sights on what the best schools would look like and how we should teach in them. Moreover, his brief text is full of real-life examples of these best practices so we know they exist, we know that they flourish, and we suspect that they incorporate aspects of the ENGAGING process.

If we choose to return to Human Development Discourse, we would teach as if each student mattered, we'd differentiate assignments and processes, we'd utilize strengths and build unified collaboration, we'd dump the standardized tests in favor of audible and visible authentic performances, we'd threaten to close the achievement gap, and we'd replace passivity and boredom with passionate exploration. Although this appears to be utopian, the fact that we have lost the vision of this kind of school should terrify you. If every moment of our careers is spent trying to increase adolescents' test scores (and ignore their persona, their character, and their dreams), we'll have given up on the joyfulness, the playfulness, and the uniqueness possible in an individual's education.

Armstrong offers a laundry list of consequences of the choices that our politicians and economic leaders have foisted on our educational leaders. These include the reversion to drill-and-kill teaching (as documented in a neat book by Linda McNeil called *Contradictions of Control*), the threat of cheating (the so-called Houston miracle whereby raised test scores turned out to be a scam comes to mind), the loss of content specialties or humanistic curriculum during the school day (and recess for the little ones), and the triumph of competitiveness over excellence. (Alfie Kohn's work has definitely shown that winning does not make for excellence, it just makes for winning.)

If we were to regain our focus, revert to our roots, and begin promoting education for true human development, Armstrong thinks the following should occur:

◆ Teenagers would actually have an education that is directly aligned to the demands of adulthood in the real world;

◆ Students would ignore labels and be able to shine, doing more of what they want or are good at;

◆ Respect for human diversity would be built on the realities of the shared and lived experience, not stifled by the demands of standardization; and

◆ Students would own their own educations.

Armstrong thinks these would be good things, and so do I.

Readers of this text should be aware that Armstrong has written a chapter on middle schools, citing the development of socioemotional and metacognitive realities as their chief goal, and one on high schools, where he cites preparation for autonomy as the prime outcome. These are excellent reviews of the purpose of adolescent education and he provides examples of places in the United States where students are thriving in the schools.

As I have done in several other places in this chapter, I will share a few quotations that illustrate both his major arguments *and* which directly link this text with the ENGAGING process. They can also be used as springboards (discussion starters) for your next chat with a colleague or as a diversion at a (boring) faculty meeting; I guarantee that they are worth your deepest reflection and I ask you to feel free to ignore my "editorial" comments in the parentheses:

- ◆ "Middle schools, or something very much like them, are needed to provide students in early adolescence with an environment that can help them negotiate the impact of puberty on their intellectual, social, and emotional lives." (p. 112) (They need to own and understand themselves.)

- ◆ "One of the tragedies of contemporary life is that no fully developed rites of passage exist for taking adolescents from childhood to adulthood." (p. 117) (He thinks contemporary school reality completely fails this requirement.)

- ◆ "...[M]ost students reported that active learning motivated them far more often than did lecture, overhead, or textbook learning." (p. 121) (There is no excellence without involvement.)

- ◆ "...[O]ne teacher who serves as mentor, advisor, counselor or guide can be instrumental for some kids to see purpose to their learning." (p. 124) (Adult relationships matter to teens.)

- ◆ "There is nothing in the current college prep rush (in secondary education) that reflects any kind of awareness at all of the need to deal with developmental tasks." (p. 139) (A teenage mind filled with academic content seems to be the ideal one that the schools want to produce.)

- ◆ "... [We should be] personalizing teaching and learning and recognizing depth over coverage." (p. 143) (This sounds like the ENGAGING process at work.)

Finally, I close this commentary by citing Armstrong's metaphors for us and our teens as we go about meeting our responsibilities in grades 5 to 12. For middle school students, he wants them to be explorers and teachers to be their *guides*. For older teens, he wants students to be *apprentices* and teachers to be their *mentors*. If we accept those roles *and* his commitment to Human Development Discourse, our work using the ENGAGING process will flourish. Students will explore, practice, investigate, exchange and ask; we will help them choose options, reinforce their attempts at understanding, praise their strengths, help them track their gains, and develop their adult roles. This sounds like a productive secondary education to me.

Note: Throughout this review, I have not once mentioned a critically important fact because Armstrong himself won't deal with it: solid, strong, meaningful, engaging, and conceptual instruction has been shown to lead to *higher* test scores (on conceptual examinations and on complex projects). This suggests that we should promote the ENGAGING process and follow his Human Development Discourse because it raises scores on good tests. He simply will not go down that path: We should practice good instruction because it is the right thing to do morally and developmentally and not recognize any legitimacy to the Academic Achievement Discourse. I am less vigilant and idealistic, more flexible, and perhaps more sensitive to political power. I would be happy to tell the policy makers that they should finance and encourage the ENGAGING process and promote the Human Development paradigm and then relax and enjoy the benefits of higher test scores as well.

Whether it is good or bad, I have attached a phrase to the end of most of the titles of my workshops and professional development sessions over the past several years: the phrase is "and increase test scores!" (I always include the exclamation point.) Add it to some of the eight ENGAGING factors and rest assured that you're moving in the right direction—and keeping both sides of the political fence happy and on board.

Three examples may help demonstrate this point:

1. Use constructivist practices like "negotiating meaning" and watch your students get excited and care about their learning—and increase test scores!

2. Create collaborative communities and watch students begin to enjoy school and embrace diversity as a strength—and increase test scores!

3. Develop note-making strategies and see teens become proud of their ideas—and increase test scores!

One more statement might suffice: "Use the ENGAGING process and see secondary students become active, interested, and productive thinkers and associates—and increase your test scores!"

Book 6

Flynn, P., Mesibov, D., Vermette, P.J., and Smith, R.M. (2004). *Applying standards based constructivism: A two-step guide for motivating middle and high school students.* Larchmont, NY: Eye On Education.

Several years ago, three long-time associates and I published a book that was attempting to translate and integrate (a) the research on human learning, (b) the theories of constructivism, and (c) actual teaching problems faced by secondary teachers. Of course, I am biased in favor of our own book—I liked it then and I like it now. Here is the original synopsis of the book that will inform you of its contents and then I will close with comments aligning its connection to the ENGAGING process.

Original Synopsis (2004)

Constructivism is a theory of learning which suggests that learners must personally work at making meaning of new ideas in light of their existing understandings; they don't absorb new ideas and information, they actually "construct" new concepts and insights. Built from the theories of Vygotsky, Dewey, Bruner, and Piaget, constructivism calls for an interactive and critical thinking approach to school content and expects students to think and collaborate to solve problems, make knowledge, and defend decisions. Constructivist practice makes all learning start with the individual student's prior knowledge and experience and is therefore able to connect every learning experience to every student, making diversity a strength in the process (Ladson-Billings, 1994).

While this may be all fine and dandy "theory," teachers are wont to ask, "So how do I do it in my classroom?" To that end, Flynn, Mesibov, Vermette, and Smith have designed the Two-Step, a model for developing and implementing constructivist lessons. In an age of high standards and standardized (high-stake) tests, it may be the only instructional approach that is effective for the diverse populations that we now teach.

The first phase, the *Exploratory*, generates an interest in the topic being examined, elicits personal understandings and prior experiences, and fosters the sharing of ideas that will allow the learners to begin to engage with new content. The interventions planned here intentionally provoke challenges to existing concepts and beliefs, thereby triggering the curiosity and confusion that fuels the drive for further inquiry. Far more complex than an anticipatory set, this phase attempts to increase intrinsic motivation, the factor that leads to quality work and deep understanding. The exploratory creates a felt need for information, creates a feeling of community, *and* validates each student's initial starting place for the next phase.

The second phase, the *Discovery*, is the place where the students do the learning/thinking work necessary to meet the clearly defined objective (or standard). Assigned a project or a task (or an assignment), the students in discovery are literally making their own meaning by completing their responsibility. The teacher strives to direct, clarify, motivate, provoke, and encourage the task engagement; in other words, the teacher facilitates the student work efforts, whether they are individual or collaborative. These interventions are crucially important because they provide feedback that is helpful, supportive, and timely—they are offered when they are most needed.

During this phase, simple rehearsal (called *practice* in many places) is *not enough:* learners must analyze, explain, transform, or do some high-level cognitive work with new information. Student thinking is audible (if they are working collaboratively) and visible, and by working the room (Konkoski-Bates, & Vermette, 2004) the teacher can catch misunderstandings as they arise, support effective processes, and assess the new knowledge developing in each learner. Shuell (2003) says that "thinking is learning" and in doing their thinking as they are doing their projects or solving their problems, the students *are* doing their learning.

In a nutshell, students *explore* a variety of ideas to get excited and ready to investigate an important piece of content and then they work to (personally) *discover* and create new ideas, generalizations, skills, and, eventually, their own meaningful understandings. Teachers facilitate the work efforts, using planned and spontaneous *interventions* to keep students thinking, focusing and reflecting. Assessment in the Two-Step is usually authentic and performance based (Wiggins & McTighe, 1998), and it can reflect a variety of formats (Gardner, 1999). Interestingly, responsibility for learning falls directly on each student (Glasser, 1986) and teachers become fully aware of the knowledge base of each adolescent so that meaningful connections and then deep understandings can be created by everyone. The result is the meeting of *standards* without the need for the standardization embedded in high-stakes, multiple-guess tests (Darling-Hammond, 1999).

Connections with the ENGAGING Factors

Since the publication of "The Case for Constructivist Classrooms" (Brooks & Brooks, 1993), the term *constructivism* has become a big deal. Naturally, arguments abound about its dangers and advantages, its meanings and its place in schools. To make a long story short, constructivism is a theory of learning (not a philosophy) that suggests that an individual learner has to actively incorporate new ideas into his or her own (unique) personal schema and use these new representations in his or her thinking. Because I hold to that theoretical stance, my job as a secondary teacher is to get teens to think deeply about important conceptual content, hoping for them to develop meaningful and useful understandings. (By the way, "remembering" stuff is a byproduct of an "understanding" focused activity, not a prerequisite. This means that concepts are the "basics," *not* facts or skills. If I may say, remembering *without* understanding is useless, and if one really understands something important, it will be difficult to forget it completely.)

Because of the tangled knot of confusion about what all of this means to classroom teachers, Flynn et al.'s text provides a systematic and user-friendly guide to developing secondary classroom activities. The Two-Step is beautiful in its simplicity and profound in its depth of application. First, the students play with ideas and past experiences that are relevant to the topic at hand, getting cognitively ready and emotionally interested to do heavy thinking and/or problem solving. Second, the students engage in authentic work that results in their individually using the new ideas in a productive fashion that forces integration with past work and is done in a manner that allows the teacher to intervene appropriately, assess the developing conceptions, and offer feedback and support to the process.

Everything in the ENGAGING process is aligned deeply with constructivist theory. The eight factors internally align to maximize intrinsic motivation, allowing students opportunities to think and rethink new content and places a premium on valuing their ideas in the social context of modern secondary school. The process is decidedly constructivist and allows teachers an infinite number of ways to implement their versions of the eight factors in specific classrooms.

Thus, I appear to be advocating the use of the Two-Step as a planning model, with the conscious use of the eight ENGAGING factors within that framework for maximum teaching effectiveness. Yes, I am doing just that and I am also suggesting that you experiment at length with this as well. The hypothetical examples offered in this text (each of the various Reallygood scenarios) follow the Two-Step structure.

Eight Research Studies That Give Evidence That We Should Examine

This section contains annotated reviews of eight key studies that were published in various journals over the past thirty years. Although they clearly offer support for the ENGAGING process, they also provide a glimpse into the world of how scholarly research does its business. In short, a question is clarified, a methodology to examine it is built and implemented in a *real and practical* setting, and an answer is established. Unlike previous centuries, the two worlds of (educational) practice and theory are now forever joined at the hip and teachers need to both critically read actual studies or reviews of some (such as those I offer here) *and* participate in research themselves. The job of a secondary teacher is increasingly more complex and this affiliation with research is one of the new and important expectations.

The reviews presented here are a nice, but totally incomplete, sampling of research related to the eight factors of ENGAGING. They deal with issues including active learning, collaboration, building community, and literacy, and they are a valuable addition to the chapter.

Research Article 1

Bargh, J.A., and Schul, Y. (1980). On the cognitive benefits of teaching. *Journal of Educational Psychology, 72*(5), 593–604.

Benware, C.A., and Deci, E.L. (1984). Quality of learning with and active versus passive motivational set. *American Educational Research Journal, 21*(4), 755–765.

This is one of those times where you get a two-for-one deal that I cannot avoid. These two pieces came out several years apart, and *changed my life!* In a nutshell, they showed that "preparing to teach something improved the individual's understanding of it as compared to preparing to take a test on that something."

Talk about a paradigm shift: This finding suggests that we should spend much of our time trying to get kids ready to "explain" new ideas and concepts and content, *not* answer test items about that very same content. Let me say it again: When students are serving in an "explainer" capacity (or role), they develop deeper understanding than when they are serving in the old-fashioned "learner" capacity (or role).

These are two studies that fully support the old adage that "the best way to learn something is to teach it to somebody else." According to Bargh and Schul, this tendency happens because preparing to teach "results in a more highly organized cognitive structure…facilitating retention of the relationships between facts and the facts themselves." Benware and Deci agree and suggest that understanding was better because the learning had a purpose and, having such, fostered more intrinsic motivation for deep understanding.

These two explanations make for a powerful rationale to use "preparing to teach" as a learning strategy. We have known this principle for a long time now; it is time to implement its meaning as fully as we can.

A quick look at that studies shows that in both, (undergraduate) students were either asked to study relatively new material for a test or prepare to teach it to someone else. Preparation time was not lengthy and was closely monitored. In both cases, the students who prepared to teach developed better and longer-lasting conceptual understanding of the target material than those who were getting ready for an exam. (They also reported higher perceptions of interest and intrinsic motivation, factors that may play a huge positive role in maintaining focus during a lengthy school year.)

Interestingly, memory for rote learning was essentially the same under both conditions. This finding, often ignored, is important in the standardized test debate: instructional approaches that take on the look of memorizing work *or* "drill-and-kill" *do not* do a better job preparing teens for even the least thoughtful and lowest level high-stakes test. Once again, when teaching for simple memory over a short time period, active and ENGAGING strategies are just as good as traditionally passive ones. But for conceptual development, there is no contest. (We all recognize that cramming for a test is equally as powerful as distributed study is in the short run, but retention over time favors distributed learning. Combing these two factors, [a] distributed engagement and [b] learning as teaching preparation, as would happen in the ENGAGING classroom, should result in great long-term conceptual gain.)

Earlier in this chapter, we met Betty Fable, a student from Perkins' (1999) article. Here are several ways that she could use the idea of "learning by preparing to teach" to its best advantage:

- ◆ After she writes the required letter in history class, she explains its key points to a classmate. She could also compare and contrast (via a Venn diagram) how her letter compares to a classmate's. Finally, she could prepare a two-minute presentation that could be videotaped by the teacher for use on Parents' Night.

- ◆ As she develops her theory about weight and velocity in physics, she can write a slogan that captures its essence and explains it to a few other students.

- ◆ In algebra, she can try her hand at writing a sentence that contrasts "simplifying an equation" with "simplifying a sentence" and prepare to handle questions about it.

- ◆ In English, she can sit in a Cooperative Learning base group and describe how the poem connects to her life and remark about how the other students have made their own connections.

Almost always, "teaching others" requires actual human conversation about real thoughts (not recitations). The transformation toward a cooperative learning community *vision* of education is well on its way at this point in time—we are well past the "sit, listen, and learn" approach to teaching.

Research Article 2

Kobayashi, Y. (1994). Conceptual acquisition and change through social interaction. *Human Development, 37*, 233–241.

Given that you are familiar with the ENGAGING process that was carefully spelled out earlier in the text, the selection of this article makes infinite sense because in this study, the researcher examines, discovers, and spells out some conditions for the construction of a permanent schema/concept change that is the whole point of formal education. Again, deep and meaningful understanding is the goal, and his work advises us to how achieve it for all teens.

In setting the context for his work, Kobayashi says two things worth quoting:

♦ "Individuals rarely generate and revise their knowledge based on propositional logic. Thus, presenting information guaranteed to be correct by authorities is not sufficient for the construction of knowledge. "(p. 234)

♦ "Children easily forget what they have discussed and observed….[I]nducing [conceptual] change takes time and varied instances of the target knowledge." (p. 239)

In the first quote, he challenges the value of the whole lecture/presentation/transmission form of teaching; in effect, he believes that while students may listen, they really do *not* change their thinking because of the words of an authority. (This is a strongly validated position.) This suggests that to learn something, they must be ENGAGED as has been described here.

The second quote challenges the ENGAGING process itself: literally, it means that the internal discoveries made by thinking teens may not be permanent after all. They may be lost if teachers do not carefully structure, sequence, and challenge teen thinking of these important insights (and concepts) over time and over differentiated content. A lesson learned may be tentative, unless it is thoughtfully rekindled, reexamined, and reflected upon. Thus, the use of strategies that require reexamination of previously learned ideas (concepts) and that require the carefully developed building of new ideas are essential to cognitive health. (This is akin to what has been called "the spiral curriculum.")

The study described here is really quite simple and yet reveals an important truth: collaborative social interaction is necessary for individual schema development. He calls this factor the "horizontal flow of information." The study demanded that students make a hypothesis about a (science) phenomenon and then exchange and share it with others (a form of cooperative learning), then change or keep their original hypothesis. They could then test their guess with an experiment or demonstration. Citing evidence that discussion causes internal disequilibrium and then sparks thoughtful attempts at reconciliation, Kobayashi emphasizes three implications of "teaching with discussion":

1. Challenges to students' original thinking (i.e. prior knowledge) are numerous and accepted in discussion;

2. Contrasting arguments are often engaged in thoughtfully while the back-and-forth interaction takes place; and

3. It easily creates an expectation for reexamination of one's ideas on a regular basis.

ALL three of these factors lead to cognitive conceptual gain.

Finally, one interesting side note comes out of this study. As posited by the ENGAGING process, a positive and supportive classroom atmosphere is directly linked to thought. Relationship building in a respectful classroom community is central to the comfortable airing of one's position for it to be argued about publicly. My point here is that this will not happen unless the teacher has a vision and a plan to deal with this issue. Students are reticent to be seen as wrong, hesitant to be seen as offering unsupported ideas, and are gun-shy about "bad guessing." Carefully developed activities that show (a) the power of developing *and* reshaping ideas against evidence, (b) the value of sharing thoughts as knowledge is formed within a community, and (c) the positive affective atmosphere of a thinking process approach is needed. Each of these requires a change in typical practice toward less "What is the single right-answer?" and more of "Why do we think that?" by teachers and students in the secondary classroom.

Research Article 3

Stodolosky, S.S., and Grossman, P.L. (2000). Changing students, changing teaching. *Teachers College Record, 102*(1), 125–172.

Contrary to my typical scholarly work, I have included in this research section a very powerful and fascinating qualitative study of "teacher change." Because I am hoping that readers of this text actually make drastic changes in their practice, share the process (and the developing findings), and reflect extensively about the effects of the changes on specific and real teenagers in their classrooms, I thought that this article might suggest that such effort is "worth it."

The authors are noted researchers whose earlier work has suggested that the content one teaches affects the changes one makes in teaching and that teacher preparation and professional development matter greatly. They find that these are still true, but that being supported by one's department and holding a clear commitment to impacting students in a desirable ways are of huge importance. I ask that you keep these in mind as you play with the ideas of this text: first, you will be better off if you are supported by associates or colleagues, get to share your experiences with them, *and* you keep a documentation of the results of your efforts on students. The latter suggestion makes you a qualitative (case study) researcher of your own classroom and, if done thoughtfully, will give you wonderful feedback about your professional development.

The study compares four high school teachers in the same school district—two math and two English. Two managed to change their practice when their students changed (they became more diverse) and the curriculum changed; two did not. The challenge to keep high expectations, to meet the needs of a diverse student body, to get every student to the new (high) standard, and to create a community of learners was (and still is) formidable. Although I suggest that using the ENGAGING process will succeed under exactly these conditions, the cases of these four teachers tells us several things that we should keep in mind.

First, that the desire to help students make connections between their lives and literature, or what I have taken to call "negotiating the meaning of the content," is central to successful adaptation to student needs (and their diversities). Less emphasis on the standard interpretations of literature and less slavish attention to the canon allows themes of real import to be examined in the classroom. A commitment to having students develop a clearly articulated personal sense of meaning makes the classroom run smoothly and keeps everyone interested.

A high sense of efficacy ("I can make change in a teen's life") is a driving force behind a teacher's ability to make this change. For those of us more fatally inclined, and who thus see ourselves as having limited impact, the study suggests that we may become discouraged and stay with our old, established strategies, despite the limited potential for success.

Interestingly, the successful English teacher (Mr. Caro) is counterpointed nicely by the other English teacher, Mr. Lawson. Amongst Lawson's distinguishing features is a comment that he does not see it as his job to "keep them from dropping out of high school." I, of course, totally dismiss this position: It is exactly his job, as teacher and advocate for every student, to convince them to study hard, to think carefully, and to take ownership of their own education *in school*! The use of the ENGAGING process that I obviously believe in, can only be achieved by highly skilled teachers and is not found on the street! Lawson is not willing to back away from past practices and continues to use his few successes as barometers to measure the failures—and lack of ability—of others.

Although committed to a critical thinking set of expectations for students, Lawson only does so in the context of "college prep." In other words, every rationale is supported by the notion that the students are doing things to get ready for college, and (my emphasis) *not because they will better understand their own worlds and their own decisions.* This is a sad and disturbing perspective—it devalues the teens' real experiences and insights, destroys attempts at community building, and negates efforts at creating thoughtful challenge. It deadens the classroom atmosphere and reduces the quantity of things that count as "quality."

Second, in the math classroom of the unsuccessful changer (Ms. Hanamori), active learning disappeared. Students did not have any discussions *and*, most importantly, were not expected to ask questions. A question-inducing strategy such as KWL (a wonderful graphic organizer) would find no place in her classrooms. Seen as distractions (or fun diversions), conceptual building activities were reduced to student-sponsored or surprise events.

Hanamori was deeply committed to the traditional model of "teacher tell, student practice," even though she had direct evidence of its dismal record with her kids. She took that data as an indicator of student lack of ability and promised *more* simple-minded practice. Her personality was one that sought organization, structure, and pattern, and she ran her classroom accordingly. Thinking was a messy business that did not fit well with her vision of a smooth operation and she totally rejected any strategies that did not place her in total control. For example, the use of manipulatives was scoffed at and she was openly hostile to cooperative learning, unless "there was an adult in every group." She did not trust the teens to think or to try, nor did she trust them to digress from a patterned format and return to it.

Those of us trying the ENGAGING process should relax and realize that we cannot learn *for* the students. The teens must think on their own for they must do the understanding. Simply put, it is their education! Teachers who fear change, who distrust "surrendering power" to students, and/or who have conceptualized understanding as memorizing a few heuristics, will neither succeed with all students nor maximize the potential of those teens committed to a highly personalized standard of excellence.

Her counterpoint, the successful changer, Mrs. Albright, saw math as a living and breathing entity that could make her students' lives a better place. Because the content was dynamic not sequential, different students could grapple with different insights at different times (and in different ways—note the use of intelligences). Notably, she also thought that education was "becoming a good citizen": developing understanding in math was directly linked to the social and emotional outcomes realized by the ENGAGING process. She sought professional development at every turn, keeping her colleagues' support for her lifetime inquiry. She was a teacher-person who could change and grow *just* as she expected her teenager-student persons to do.

Clearly, in both sets of teachers, the one who changed to meet student needs is the one who aligns well with the ENGAGING process. But an interesting phenomenon may lay at the bottom of this juxtaposition and centers on this question: What is the key role of the secondary teacher?

The most effective answer to that question seems to revolve around some aspect of motivating students to learn. As a dedicated constructivist, I realize that there may be many potentially good answers but Stodolosky and Grossman point out that Albright and Caro, like those embracing ENGAGING, see themselves as searchers for motivational strategies that will help students to develop conceptual meaning *and* take control of their thinking. Everything from "using grades judiciously," which is set to keep students hopeful and optimistic for success, to building a collaborative community, which is meant to crush the competitive structure that destroys effort and limits excellence, is designed to foster the pursuit of understanding in an emotionally upbeat manner. School works when thinking is intentional, evidence is thoughtful, and the spirit is joyful for each student. Creating that environment is the underlying goal of successful teachers.

Research Article 4

Spires, H.A., and Donley, J. (1998). Prior knowledge activation: Inducing engagement with informational texts. *Journal of Educational Psychology*, *90*(2), 249–260.

There are two major reasons that this article was selected from the hundreds of pieces of reading research that are available. First, like dozens of articles that would be found in any quick search, this one has the word "engaging" in the title. Second, this study, conducted on ninth graders in real classrooms with real texts, demonstrates a result that is important to teachers who are seriously considering a shift toward conscious implementation of the eight ENGAGING factors.

It appears that everyone wants instruction to be "engaging" and for students to be "engaged." This may well end up offering a lot of reminders and advertisements for this text, but it also suggests that the word has many meanings. Although Spires and Donley do *not* define their use of the term, it can be inferred from their study that "reading engagement" means that teens are seeking personal connections to and meanings for the information in the narrative they are assigned. Moreover, by calling up their own prior relevant information, they are creating contexts for new ideas. Thus, (reading) engagement seems to suggest willful, personal, and thoughtful connections to passages in text (which, by the way, I have just done here!). Although not a complete advertisement for my version of ENGAGING, it certainly seems that they have applied its core meaning to reading.

Additionally, by dealing with the type of texts that teens will be actually exposed to during their own studies, the authors have created a transferable setting from which teachers can modify their own practice. Following a lengthy explanation of the scholarship on reading, their two action research studies recognize the "constructivist" and "reader response" approaches and seemingly reject the traditional notion that reading uncovers a "static" message, an approach they refer to as "referential meaning." Within that active learning context, they examine conditions that called for students to do one of the following: (a) just read, (b) read for main ideas, or (c) read while commenting from personal perspectives. They also combine categories b and c. Ninth graders were taught these strategies and then asked to use them. Postinstruction testing included free response (what they understood and recalled) and forced choice (choose from given alternatives). It revealed that the more active approach using, prior knowledge activation (PKA) improved student understanding and improved attitudes toward reading. (This PKA strategy is often helped when it is combined with a process that forces students to find the main idea; however, main idea alone is not as powerful as PKA alone.) In short, teachers who get students to use reading strategies that call for personalized "negotiated meaning" as they read *textbooks* will have more successes. Obviously, these are powerful and notable results, and ones that are consistent with the ENGAGING process.

The authors offer three other points worth quoting here:

◆ "Personal connections during reading fostered higher level thinking about the text." (p. 257)

◆ "The inclusion of personal knowledge is inherently more motivating than the relatively low-interest task of extracting main ideas." (p. 257)

◆ "The notion of text engagement must be expanded from simply a cognitive construct to one that includes and interests to students." (p. 257)

In short (again), when students' negotiated meaning is considered appropriate, useful, and valued by teachers and peers, attitudes and understanding increase. Building a community that respectfully listens to and reacts to everyone's ideas is a community that will make schooling productive for all learners.

Application (A Closing)

Often, my Niagara students grasp the types of ideas made in this review but have moderate difficulty "applying" the researchers' findings to real classrooms, lacking both the prior experience and the right context to be productive. To help move this process, I offer this exercise, drawn from social studies, to give the you a chance to experience the "reader response with personal connections" intervention that Spires and Donley designed.

As you read this paragraph from Shenkar's (2006) *The Chinese Century*, use the righthand column to write down anything you recall about the topic *and* any personal commentary you have about the topic.

Passage	Response
Chinese firms are not the only ones to engage in anything from the copying of art design to industrial espionage. It is the scale, the scope, and brazenness that set China apart and create an impact of major proportions. Although rankings are unavailable, various indicators point at China as the undisputed leader in the use, manufacturing, distribution and exportation of pirated and counterfeit products. (p. 86)	

Although the whole point of Response is for you to make your own connections, I cannot easily debrief your thinking right now. However, I do offer several comments from various people who have done this activity in a classroom-type setting. Their statements may help you see the variety and depth of active thinking that engaged reader's experience.

- ♦ "Is the scale of this process so big because China is so big?"
- ♦ "I have never bought anything bogus from any place."
- ♦ "Wonder which other countries rank highly?"
- ♦ "Funny, I never thought of a country as being 'brazen.' Usually, I only think of that word with some arrogant, cocky, tough guy."
- ♦ "Mike's firm makes interesting equipment. I wonder if they think about espionage at all?"
- ♦ "Does the United States have laws about stealing ideas?"

This sampling shows personal commentary, reflective questioning, and concept clarification about the content of Chinese economics. Thinking these things places the reader *inside* of the content, where the reader belongs (and needs to be). Although using this strategy slows down the reading process, it increases efficiency and (eventually) becomes internalized and used more quickly.

I close with this old maxim: "In the student-centered classroom, the teacher does, indeed, think about content. But he or she is thinking about what the students are thinking about the content…and how to respond."

Spires and Donley have shown us that "student-centered" reading of narrative texts, and showing respect for student written and verbal documentations of said text, improves understanding and enthusiasm for school. One could safely say that engagement with texts aligns with engagement in class. Teens should matter enough for us to experiment with this easily used approach.

Research Article 5

> Schwartz, D.L., and Bransford, J. (1998). A time for telling. *Cognition and Instruction, 16*(4), 475–522.

This is a crucially important piece of research for two reasons:

1. It provides *no* support for the traditional teaching practice conceptualized as information dissemination or pure lecture. By itself, lecture does little to spark the cognitive processes necessary for meaningful understanding to occur.

2. However, when combined with prior activities (especially ones that force students to make distinctions between things), a great deal of learning by listening to a formal lecture presentation can take place.

The difference, of course, seems to be in the "getting ready to learn" phase that comes before the information is shared.

To quote the authors, "…in telling [without] readiness, the recourse for students is to treat new information as ends to be memorized, not as tools to help them think." The so-called lecture-*after*-generating-distinctions approach is apparently the more productive condition because it offers evidence for the meanings thinkers are in the process of making.

In a prior work, associates and I have argued for an Exploratory phase as a prerequisite to students beginning work on a project or an authentic task (see Flynn et al., 2004). Such a phase meets Schwartz and Bransford's criteria perfectly: They make the student actively analyze relevant content, motivating them to seek the very information that the teller wishes to tell. In terms of the ENGAGING process, there are several clear factors whose use prepares the student to productively receive "new" information that can be easily internalized.

First, the use of graphic organizers and note-taking strategies force students to encode and analyze new ideas in terms of their own prior structures, readying them to integrate any new ideas that are presented to them.

Second, the whole point of negotiating meaning requires that the students *do* something cognitive with the newly received information: Making a personal interpretation, comparing it to an example or an analogy, or transforming it into one's own "story" demonstrates what was heard and learned and provide opportunities for feedback and/or further scaffolding. Moreover, the use of collaborative discussion of interesting case studies, a staple of many engaging classes, results in student interpretations, student hypotheses, and/or student insights, any of which would prepare students to effectively attend to the messages offered by the teacher.

Finally, many of us talk about "hands-on" activities and confuse physical movement with cognitive processing. "Minds-on" is a more powerful metaphor than is "hands-on," implying that activities that create confusion, or spark interest, or force distinctions, or prompt a cry for an answer will be met with verbal explanations (telling) that will be actively processed—ideas from such a lecture will be analyzed, connected, assessed, critiqued, and/or immediately used to solve a problem and result in deep and applicable understanding.

In sum, the three individual experiments involved in this article were beautifully designed to compare the readiness impact of a task that forced students to actively *generate* distinctions and then hear (or read) new information with ones that offered (a) reading about distinctions + hearing a lecture, (b) summarizing a text + hearing a lecture, or (c) two-generation activities. In each case, college students had a week between doing the primary activity and making predictions about future applications. In each comparison, the generating distinctions + telling group outscored the other variable on the conceptual test used as a dependent measure: Listening to a lecture or hearing a presentation telling *after* becoming ready (for the information) was the most powerful of the three conditions tested.

Research Article 6

Vermette, P. (1994). Four fatal flaws: Avoiding the common mistakes of novice users of cooperative learning. *The High School Journal*, 255–260.

It is pretty obvious that I am very familiar with this article and a subsequent text on the topic of Cooperative Learning entitled *Making Cooperative Learning Work* (Vermette, 1998) since I wrote them both. I have perhaps made a dubious decision to enter this article in the research section of the book because it represents (a) a translation of a highly technical study into user-friendly English and (b) still offers a valuable piece of advice. It is *not* a classic "research report," which I suspect will make some readers very happy. It does, however, paint the picture of my study *and* offers four useful suggestions that have stood the test of time.

I have been studying Cooperative Learning since a time before many of you were born and the research base is absolutely clear: Cooperative Learning works for cognitive gain in secondary classrooms. There is just no doubt about its potential usefulness. However, many teachers have not liked it, have not tried it, have not examined it, and/or have not implemented it well. Let me, therefore, change my generalization to this: "Well-structured and thoughtful Cooperative Learning works for cognitive gain *and* social-emotional development in secondary classrooms."

Moreover, I have not yet met a single teacher who has played with Cooperative Learning, experimented with it, tweaked it, *and* given up on it. My good friend, Cindy Kline has become an expert in its use in middle school Spanish because she has a deep understanding of its form and structure, knows what she expects from it, and is willing to reflect on her practice with it. Every teacher's version of Cooperative Learning is his or her own adaptation (see Siegel, 2005), and yet I make four strong suggestions to anyone using this for the first time:

1. The teacher should build the groups or assign the partners. So, in the beginning, don't let them pick their workmates. If you do, they will find friends (Mitchell et al., 2000), avoid unfamiliar or low-status classmates, or avoid social outcasts/isolates, and then not work very diligently. Heterogeneous groups benefit everyone and teachers must *explain* this to students because they typically will not seek diverse relationships without being expected to do so.

2. The first task should be carefully constructed to insure "positive interdependence" and to maximize chances for success. Essentially, it must be done during classroom time and debriefed for (a) the quantity of content-learning, (b) the quality of social interaction, and (c) individuals' perceptions of their effort and contribution. "Processing-out" (Johnson & Johnson, 1999), a discussion of the actual interaction, is vital; students must start to see their own thinking and interpret their interactive behaviors. Clearly, how teens work with diverse others and their ability to communicate effectively are central to a teen's developing "work" skills; corporations in a global economy and a diverse society demand this from their employees (Kline & Vermette, 2006). In fact, it may be a contemporary "basic" skill of the modern world: thoughtful Cooperative Learning gives students a rich experience with it.

3. The third suggestion is to use some class time for students to do their work together, especially when "big team projects" are involved. When teamwork is conducted in class, the teacher can

see and assess the growth, the individual contributions, the quality of interaction and can intervene to rectify misconceptions or trouble-shoot misunderstandings. The teacher also can identify any "parasites" (free riders) who are tempted to let others work for him or her. When learning is "visible and audible," teachers can help.

4. The fourth suggestion is to fight the temptation to "group grade" every teamed product. While it is simple to do this, and it appears to be "fair," the strategy can be abused and can lead to deep resentment (especially among high achievers). I suggest that you come up with a system that balances group work and individual gain *and* discuss the rationale for it with the teens before they start work.

Glance at the title again. The four fatal flaws are embedded in the suggestions offered. Here they are again in a new form: If you let them pick their own workmates, have them do a complex and lengthy project outside of classroom time, and group grade the product, you will effectively *kill* the chance to gain the benefits of Cooperative Learning. (As a matter of fact, if you do those four things, you'll be doing *groupwork*, not Cooperative Learning.)

Use of the ENGAGING process envisions careful collaborations between students *and* a sense of a supportive, encouraging, and interactive "learning" community. This means Cooperative Learning must become a staple of the teacher's practice. Clearly, in well-structured Cooperative Learning classes, students maximize the opportunities to make their own meanings, document their cognitive and social experiences, and increase the likelihood that they develop appreciation for diversities.

This final point about diversities includes multiple-intelligences style interventions. Working together on increasingly complex tasks (Cohen, 1994) allows students to see and feel how other teens' talents, interests, and skills complement their own. The successful adult world needs everyone's differential contribution, and shows the teens that each of them does *matter*.

For an 11-year-old or an 18-year-old, peer respect, peer support, and positive peer relationships are a staple to identity development and meaningful cognitive gain—thoughtful and well-structured Cooperative Learning allows this to happen.

Research Article 7

Osterman, K. (2000). Students' need for belonging in the school community. *Review of Educational Research, 70*(3), 323–367.

The journal holding this study, *Review of Educational Research*, is noted for two things: (a) it is the premier publishing location for scholars who have studied the available research on a topic or issue, and (b) it is thoroughly respected and, to many, including me, seems to offer the definitive voice on a topic. When Osterman got her review published in *Review of Educational Research*, it was time to take notice.

Osterman simply asked three questions, including the key (*essential*) one: "How important is a sense of belonging in an educational setting?" Her answer, after sorting, evaluating, and categorizing hundreds of individual studies, is "very important." She says, "Students who experience acceptance are more highly motivated and *engaged* in learning and more committed to school" (p. 359).

That is a pretty clear call to attention. Here are a few ideas from the article.

1. Without a sense of belongingness, students find "diminished motivation, impaired development, alienation, and poor performance." Teens in school learn within the context of the classroom and school environment. If the community is *not* supportive, a teen will find it very difficult to persist and seek excellence. To quote her again, "sense of belonging influences achievement through its effects on engagement."

2. A supportive teacher–student relationship manifests itself in a student's perception of his or her own competence. Teachers must find ways to encourage and promote the efforts of individual learners; these expressions of caring lead to internal acceptance and ownership of one's own education.

3. "Middle school seems to be a crucial time, especially for boys." School is more important than family on this issue. Peer acceptance and what I'll call "comfort in school" are mandatory for avoiding alienation in the middle level. Calls for the development of a clear approach to social emotional learning, such as is mentioned by Battistich et al. (1995), Elias and Arnold (2006), and by Armstrong (2006), are right on target. I use the phrases "group for collaboration" and "build relationships and community" to capture these expectations. Teens, especially boys, cannot learn academic content in either an emotional vacuum or a social prison. This last point is one that Osterman dwells on appropriately. Much previous research has been on the student–teacher relationship; outside of Cooperative Learning scholarship, there are few sources on student–student relationship building. But the Cooperative Learning literature is clear: it works well on the emotional lives of teens. Secondary teach-

ers should be highly skilled at its structure and in its implementation for both cognition and social interaction.

4. Finally, this review also mentions that teachers' sense of belonging *also* "matters." "Collegiality is one of the most important organizational features influencing sense of efficacy, and professional commitment." Do yourself a favor: find someone at school to talk with about this book, perhaps focusing first on this article. Share your insights, critiques, and hesitations. Share your attempts at implementing the eight ENGAGING factors and, especially, your thoughtful innovations regarding community building. Despite media portrayals of "Lone Ranger" teachers changing teens before the principal sees it, most of us do our work in conjunction with, and in relation to, our colleagues. Tonto had the Lone Ranger, and vice versa; they needed each other to maximize their individual impacts. We do, too.

Research Article 8

Woloshyn, V.E., Pavio, A., and Pressley, M. (1994). The use of elaborative interrogation to help students acquire information consistent with prior knowledge and information inconsistent with prior knowledge. *Journal of Educational Psychology, 86,* 79–89.

Much has been done in the study of the role of prior knowledge to human learning. As recently as 2004, Shapiro did a study that informed researchers that prior knowledge was even more important than previously thought. Wow! I didn't think that was possible: Everything new has to be integrated into existing structures or schema (something old). We cannot learn anything new without connecting it directly with our prior knowledge. "Calling up prior knowledge" is a staple of most books on instructional design. What is left to teachers, though, is a sense of how to do that often, accurately, with diverse students, and for various concepts. Handling that challenge is why they pay us the big bucks!

I offer that careful use of the ENGAGING process really maximizes the actual thinking done by individual students, which automatically utilizes prior knowledge. For example, a student cannot write a sentence about what she thought about a poem without using her own vocabulary, her own images, and her own emotions. Likewise, if I were to ask you what you make of the following sentence, what would you say?

From a position in front of Lee, Kim gave Chris her three books.

The words are clear, the parts of the sentence are there, but I am not sure if I have just communicated my meaning to you. Meaning making is in your own mind and your prior knowledge and experience lead you in the direction of an interpretation (any ambiguity is in the receiver, not in the information). Whose books did Chris get? How many of these people are female? Where is Kim? How many people are there at the scene?

The authors took a hard look at middle schoolers' ability to process existing knowledge with new information, using elaboration techniques (like I've advocated here) to help. (Control groups did a traditional reading assignment.) Some statements-to-learn they faced challenged their existing beliefs; others supported or were consistent with them. In each case, they were asked to respond to the fact with their own answer to a *why* question: "Why is this fact true?"

A few examples of true statements may help you see their structure.

1. In space, the sun's heat cannot even roast a potato.

4. Oxygen is not the same as air.

23. Earthworms come in many colors including brown, green, and purple.

31. Some living things have only one cell.

There were thirty-two statements altogether. After each statement, the students answered the *why* question in writing.

Here is what the study showed:

1. If the new fact was a challenge to their existing beliefs, the answering of the *why* question helped them remember the true answer. (It did not get mixed up with their old understandings. They could learn new, challenging information by "playing with it," to use my friend Ted Werner's language.)

2. In terms of remembering the facts, the quality of the answer to the *why* question did not matter as much as the active attempt to derive an answer! This is evidence that active problem solving does focus attention and increase remembering.

3. The gains from activity were still present after six months. This type of cognitive activity limited forgetting.

4. Students who were placed in the control group (which just read the statements) were far more likely to act surprised and challenged the correctness of the new facts; they also didn't retain their *trueness* very long.

5. Memory for new knowledge that was consistent with existing beliefs was greater than for inconsistent beliefs. Prior knowledge matters!

In closing, this complicated study is a good representation of how the knowledge base is built by research. The authors took a couple of studies, discovered a related-but-as-of-yet-unanswered question, set up a study, and conducted it. They did not answer all the questions possible about "elaborative interrogation questions," but they did get data that could serve as evidence of their (new) beliefs.

◆ The type, not just the amount of, prior knowledge matters to teens as they meet new ideas.

◆ Constructing his or her own answers to a *why* question matters to a teens' recall *and* understanding.

Research has brought forth these generalizations; they are amongst the many research findings that are clearly consistent with the type of suggestions offered by the ENGAGING process.

Pseudoexam

Directions: Each of the following statements is true and relates directly to one of the readings that you have just finished. Mark it true, *and then* answer the question, "*Why* is it true?," in the space provided. (Yes, this is exactly what the subjects did in the last study reviewed in the chapter, the study by Woloshyn, Pavio, and Pressley [1994].) There are no tricks—these are true statements (according to the texts reviewed).

_____ 1. Black children are more likely to thrive cognitively when the teacher uses a "mining" approach like discussion than when the teacher uses a "banking" approach like drill or lecture (Ladson-Billings, 1994).

Question: Why is this true?

_____ 2. When students construct an authentic project, there are a number of ways that they can design it that are equally valid indicators of their deep understanding (Gardner, 2006; Tomlinson & McTighe, 2006).

Question: Why is this true?

_____ 3. When facing new content, teens are better off preparing to teach it to someone else than they are studying it for an examination (Bargh & Schul, 1980; Benware & Deci, 1984).

Question: Why is this true?

_____ 4. Thoughtful use of structured Cooperative Learning increases conceptual achievement, helps teens like school, and helps teens like themselves better (Vermette, 1994).

Question: Why is this true?

_____ 5. Building community that provides teens with a sense of belonging and tying it to high academic expectations maximizes teenagers' achievement and their attitudes toward other people and to school (Ostermann, 2000).

Question: Why is this true?

_____ 6. Carefully structured reading assignments, ones that force students to personally elaborate and/or analyze the material, increase teen understanding of new content (Woloshyn, Pavio, & Pressley, 1994; Spires, & Donley, 1998).

Question: Why is this true?

_____ 7. Most teens think that most of school is mostly boring, but they do realize that they thrive and learn a lot when they're engaged in active learning (Armstrong, 2006).

Question: Why is this true?

4

Begin at the Beginning: Putting ENGAGING into Action

Essential Questions

What do other successful educators say about engagement, cognition, and teen learning? How do I get started? What else should I be aware of?

This final chapter attempts to do several things as it closes out the text. First, it offers some suggestions about getting started with implementation of the ENGAGING process. We start with the first day of school for three first-year math teachers. Their decisions will set the framework and expectations for how their classrooms will run, and they have the opportunity to sell the teens on ENGAGING practices at the most opportune time. Most of us will start our own experimentations in the middle of the year, but reflecting on how the groundwork can be laid for its use at the outset may help us. Missed opportunities are easier to see in other's work than in one's own, and so we can learn by studying other's decisions.

E	entice effort
N	negotiate meaning
G	group collaboratively
A	active learning
G	graphic organizers
I	intelligence interventions
N	note making
G	grade wisely

Next, you will read about three successful secondary teachers and their attempts to engage teens and create a supportive environment. They epitomize the best of our profession and their stories should inspire us. These veterans are experts on building relationships and fostering community and they have been ENGAGING diverse teens' minds for more than fifty years. There is much to borrow from them as you settle on changes that you wish to play with in your own practice. (In many ways, these three have served as models of great ENGAGING work and they are to be thanked for their commitment to our teens and our futures.)

Third, we take another brief look at Cooperative Learning, as an instructional strategy and as an organizing structure. Typically, well-developed Cooperative Learning is the most powerful instructional strategy that educators have devised so far. Careful and thoughtful use of Cooperative Learning will help all teachers (and teens) meet their goals. Furthermore, "group collaboratively" is not only a basic tenet of ENGAGING, but is also a central feature of all social constructivist classrooms. Productive student–student interaction is likely the least tapped resource that contemporary teachers use effectively. The reluctance to have teens dialogue with each other may come from many sources, but overcoming that hesitancy is a key step to maximizing the ENGAGING process.

Fourth, we will take some time to contrast two meanings of the term *practice* a word every teacher likes but uses differently. By setting *practice* in two differing paradigms, we can assess the impact it has on teen ENGAGEMENT.

Fifth, we take a look at the Reallygoods, a coteaching middle school couple who collaborate on learning tasks and who have their students do likewise. As this example demonstrates, carefully developed projects can help students take ownership of their own thinking, the most desirable outcome predicted by use of the ENGAGING factors.

Finally, the Six Facets of Understanding, as developed by Wiggins and McTighe (2005), may give us new ways to use active and authentic assessment to differentiate students' cognitive growth and increase their affective commitment. We touched on it earlier (it was summarized in Chapter 3), and we will use it here to help you more fully integrate the journey you have taken with this book into your regular daily work.

Starting a Math Career:
The First Day of Misses X, Y, & Z

Three first-year math teachers are facing their first days as secondary teachers in a beautiful suburban Virginia secondary school on a glorious late summer morning. Lee High School has 1,450 ethnically diverse students, most of whom are children of middle or upper-middle class parents who wish for an enriched classroom environment and eventual college acceptance for their kids. The twenty-five ninth graders in the three rooms are also in their first days at the school and see themselves as "pretty typical and OK" young Americans. Several are math "whizzes" and more than a couple hate math, fear it, and dislike it "even more than social studies," to use one girl's words. Each of the young female teachers is between 24 and 28 years old, is in her first professional teaching assignment, and is a white northerner. (These women did not student teach in this region, but were recruited by the district for this school.)

As you peruse the three descriptions, please compare and contrast the events and actions that take place in their first period classrooms. You may wish to use a Venn diagram to record your insights, organizing and making visible the similarities and the unique properties of each case.

Miss X

The forty-eight minutes of class were marked by several distinct chunks of activities and tasks. The first fifteen minutes were devoted to her explanations of the class rules and stressed her commitment to enforcing them fairly and quickly. She gave a no-nonsense attitude of confidence, control, and power. There would be no tardiness, no talking unless called on, no note passing, no daydreaming, and no picking on each other. "This is my classroom—this is my class—and you'll learn math and respect."

She also really stressed the role of student homework as part of their responsibilities for the course. "I assign it everyday, collect it everyday, and read it over everyday. It counts for 40% of your grade and there are no lates accepted. It must be on my desk *before* the bell rings to start class. Any questions?" There were none.

The second part of class was focused on the math that was to be done in the course. Miss X handed out a sample problem sheet with five questions. "Do your best, eyes on your own work, no calculators needed. You have ten minutes." With that, she walked around, smiling, praising several students for their work, pointing to a specific part on three students' papers, and quietly muttering to herself. Near the end she gave a two-minute warning and offered this advice: "Some of you are really bad at this math. Question 5 is supposed to be missed, but many of you guys are messing up on the first two;

didn't you pass last year in eighth grade? Get ready to really work hard unless you are okay with failing."

Those comments brought about three loud groans from boys seated in the back. Immediately, Miss X gave them a dirty sneer and suggested that they be quiet, get to work, and find a new place to sit tomorrow. "I will be watching you," she commented.

When she called time, she used the front board to demonstrate an "easy" way to solve each of the problems. After each of her explanations, she asked if anyone had problems with it. Happily, only a few kids admitted that they had trouble with any of them, mostly the final one. "Good," Miss X said, "we're ready to go."

Finally, the last part of class was used to cover the book with brown paper and get the stamped numbers recorded in her Master Book. Students were given an assignment, and a suggestion to get started: "Remember what I said. Tonight, you only have eight problems from chapter 1 to do. Use your time wisely. Page 4 will be helpful."

As the bell rang and the first group left, Miss X reclined and relaxed a little in her chair and let some air blow out of her lungs. She thought that she had kept control, started their work, discovered some personalities, and not given a detention (as she had thought she'd have to do.) "Pretty good day," she muttered as she stood to watch the next class enter.

Miss Y

As the bell rang, Miss Y left her post at the door and finished her discussion (about the weather) with a small girl in the back. "Gotta get us going," she chirped and smiled as she said to all: "Class—eyes up here, please. I am Miss Y. I am a new math teacher here. I am originally from New Jersey and already love this town. I have heard how smart this new class is and am excited to be your teacher. As you know, math is critical to everyday life and we are going to learn to use it to our advantage. I have this big chart up here [she points to a huge sheet of butcher paper over her desk] with two columns. One is to keep track of how math helps us all the time and the other is for how math only matters in school. Real life—school life. It'll be fun to keep track. Now, please get out a piece of paper and put your name on it. This is your first quiz and you should get an A on it."

As the students scrambled to get the paper, she noticed two boys who did not move. She brought each paper and a pencil and offered it to them, quietly saying, "You can bring your own stuff tomorrow." Another nonmoving student was encouraged to get equipment from another student and was directed to say "thanks." She did both.

"First take the index card on the desk, fold it and put your name on it so I—and everyone else—can use your name properly. Inside the fold write three things about you that are pretty neat, or special, or interesting. Hurry. Then number the paper from one to five. You have one minute to write down all the ways that math connects to this classroom. Go." A cacophony began and she ignored it. "Write them down, I want to collect them."

At the end of the minute, she spoke again. "Now, number from six to fifteen; you have eight minutes to do this task. Go around the room and find what other people have said and borrow it on to yours. Please say please, use the person's name, and I thank you for saying thank you. Moreover, record the person's name who assisted you. Do not write anything that you cannot explain. For example, if I wrote that the windows show ninety-degree angles, and I got it from Marge, I would have to be able to explain what that meant. And yes, of course, you must talk to do this." Looking at a name card, she then says, "Robert, what is the task?" Robert responds adequately and she smiles, nods, and puts them to work.

During the work time, she wanders and listens carefully to the numerous student exchanges. She also glances at the name tags, peeking to see what they had written on the inside part. She sees no student disrespect and does see several examples of the type of kidding around that goes with good friends. Only one student, Kaina, seems "isolated" and reluctant to engage with others. Miss Y notices that sports examples play a large role for many students, mostly males. They have noticed the baseball and soccer posters, the photos of stadiums, and the sheet of baseball statistics. Many students seem to be laughing as they try to find out what the others mean by their answers. Three black students (out of the nine visible minorities in class) have noted that there is a timeline of African-American History on the back wall. Miss Y also notices that no students have noticed the clock, the posted school day time schedule, the low hum of music in 4/4 time on the radio (set to 1500AM), the equally stacked piles of books, or the rectangular shape of the room itself. "These will be added later," she thought, and it made her more deeply understand that most math is invisible to most citizens.

"OK, please stop. Before I collect these, I want to tell you that we will be doing a lot of fun and interesting math stuff and I am sure that every one of you will get through the SOL [Virginia's standards of learning] exam without a problem. We have to work together and you should be very proud of how you collaborated, helped each other, questioned things you didn't understand, and were not afraid to meet new folks. *Great!*" With that, she applauded them, and they joined in. It took a good twenty seconds to get the room quiet again.

"Please draw these two things for me right now. Listen carefully and then you can chat with someone near you, but work to your best ability. First, *draw* this: there is fifty percent, two quarter pieces, of the key lime pie left after dinner. Please cut that into halves [she waits a few seconds]. Second, Jake runs four miles due east from the school, then three miles south where he meets up with Daneeka and they run back to his starting place." She does not repeat the directions or specifics but does let the students exchange interpretations. They work through their confusions and many appear befuddled. Then, with a few minutes left she speaks again, "Math is often about figuring out things. In the first example, you might notice that you now have four pieces of pie left. That is, you divided something (two somethings) by a half and got four. Do you see it? That is a very difficult thing for most people to grasp. By the end of the week, each of you'll be able to explain it." Her statement was met by great outcries, mostly from people cheering that they got it, and only a few moaning that they hadn't. "Hold it down, we'll have to have some rules to make this class thing work for everybody. We can make the rules we'll need later this week. In the other drawing, you'll note that Jake ran farther than Daneeka and they both ran five miles back to school. Is that right?" A hush fell over class, and a few hands shot up. "Margaret, Kaina, Jon, Bryan, Tackster—Tackster?—Sasheen, Holden. Explain your interpretations to others around you. Listen to them for a minute."

This presented itself as a strange scene: six groups of kids showing and examining the thinking processes of some of their own.

With several minutes to go, Miss Y announces the homework. "Tonight, talk to your parents or neighbors—not to other students, adults are better for this—about these two drawings. Find out their 'takes' and be ready to share. And, oh yeah, fill this out now or overnight, but you have to have it ready before class. Homework counts as extra points and everybody needs extra points." With that, she distributed the outslip with four stems for day 1:

1.   One thing that got me going in class today was…

2.   The hardest thing about math is…

3.   When Miss Y says, "Math is everywhere," she means…

4.   Dividing by ½ and dividing by 2 are…

The bell rings, Y shakes a few hands, sweeps the name cards and the students' papers into an oversized bag, and says, "See you tomorrow," to the leaving herd. Her thoughts revolve around the amount of student-based information she has taken in and curiosity about what they've written about the room.

Miss Z

Miss Z begins class just as the bell rings and students respond by scrambling to a nearby seat. "Please grab a chair and pay attention for a minute. Thanks."

She sits on the desk and smiles, "I am Miss Z and I am your new teacher. I am from Boston and am glad to be here. I loved my student teaching. I love math and the Washington Redskins. And now I am part of your life. Please think of one thing that everyone should know about you and be ready to tell us all."

Ten seconds later she points to a student in front: "I am Bill. I went to Oceanside Middle School last year and am new here. I don't know anybody."

"Thanks, Bill. Next?"

A large, hulking brown-skinned young woman stands up and speaks softly, "I am Moneesha and I really hate math. I don't see why I gotta learn it; I ain't never gonna use it. Oh yeah, and I like dogs."

It takes about 25 minutes for the introductions and frankly, few students pay attention to each other. One response ("I got grounded and then home schooled last year") was met with laughter and it was the only time that Miss Z intervened. "No making fun of each other, OK? I have only three rules: be nice to everyone, do your work, and think quietly. Anybody got a problem with that?" When no one did, they went on.

Among the other introductions were one that was done in mime, that Z found a little annoying, and one that was done in Spanish and caused seven other students to roll their eyes. Miss Z couldn't help but think of Escalante and wondered if she was "stand and deliver" material.

After the introductions, Z told more about herself: "I like math for several reasons: many good jobs come from math and I love that I am qualified for them."

"Second, in math, there is one right answer and I love to know that I did something the right way. Life is simpler without lots of choices and confusions. You hang with me and I'll show you how to do all of the problems in this text [as she waves the book in front of her]. Everybody can remember math formulas and solve these problems."

"Third, math can be fun. There is eloquence to the patterns and if you can see them, well, there is beauty, too. Math is beautiful and pleasurable, as you will find out. For example, the symmetry of a butterfly is really a neat thing. Now, grab a book from the rack and turn to page 4."

It takes about five minutes for everyone to be ready and here is how the last few minutes are used: "On page 4 are some problems. You should be able to solve some correctly right now and all of them by the end of next week's first *big* test. Pick any one and try it out right now."

With one minute left, she grabs the chalk and says, "Look at problem #3. Here is what you need to know." With that she quickly bangs out a solution in full public view of everyone. "OK? Any questions? That was an easy one. Do six more for homework and we'll go over them at the start of class tomorrow. Please get your book covered at home. You are big kids now and you know how to do it. On your way out, there is a stack of handouts by the door. That sheet is called 'all about the course.' Read it over and we'll discuss it later. Have a good day." At that instant, the bell rang and the students began filing out while Miss Z dutifully erased the solution set from the board. Her thoughts left the rushed business at the end and lingered on the various introductions.

Authors' Comments

These are three very different young teachers, making different decisions that will have huge impacts as their effects ripple through the next 180 days in their individual classroom communities. In terms of examining their use of the ENGAGING process, I wish to point out a few key factors that you may also have noted as you read.

First, although there is much to contrast in the three scenarios, the biggest difference is how the teachers viewed the roles of the students. Whereas Miss X saw them as recipients of fixed knowledge, Miss Z saw them as individuals who needed information and training in math thinking; only Miss Y saw them as real thinkers and investigators who had to develop their own new meanings for math-related activities. She tried to ENGAGE them at their own unique levels and tried to foster a sense of classroom community. Her use of the six teens to "share with and teach others" is fundamentally different from how the other two teachers see teens.

Here is another way to see this factor: Without any students, Miss X's class would look pretty much the same. They are not central to her work. She presents the material; they receive it (if they want). Without students present, Z's class would lose the lengthy but useless ice-breaker introductions (that actually worked against building community) and would focus on her showing a few problems (and assigning more for practice). Without students, Miss Z could not teach; they and their thoughts are the medium in which she operates. Most of her comments either get students work-thinking or they are comments on what students had just experienced; while predictable patterns exist, no class, no activity is ever "scripted."

While X and Z are essentially "information givers," only Miss Y is a "thought provoker," or ENGAGER.

Second, the expectations for written work, what is called "note making" in this book, is also notably different for Y. Most teachers want teens to write down the key things that teachers say (and are written on the board). Y forces them to document their own thinking, which can be useful to them later (as they reflect) and to her immediately (as she assess their understanding).

Note also how Miss Y utilizes a graphic organizer, the T-bar, to keep a permanent class record of their insights. "Math matters: real life vs. school life" will grow all year and be a reminder of the journey the class community is taking together.

Finally, it is only the first day of school, but one does wonder how these teachers will *grade* their students. (The students are wondering about this as well.) Truthfully, Miss X appears to be a "catcher," a teacher who enjoys finding mistakes in student work. Correcting these mistakes usually means trying to fix a deficiency, a process that often makes students feel defensive, incompetent, and damaged. Fred Newman's (1992) work shows that this type of feeling leads to alienation and is central to the decision to "give up" and "stop trying" by high school students. His words "estrangement, detachment, isolation" seem to be accurate descriptors of some of our students' moods.

Miss Z may be setting students up to be successful by enjoying their math work and by seeing its beauty in common aspects of life. She tells them that they can all do it, even if they had trouble on that very first day. However, her comment about "one right answer" as one of the great things about math should trouble us all: It suggests that she wants them all to be the same and get the correct answer in the one correct way she offers them. Thus, her class may provide a training experience, not a thinking one; her testing and assessment process will likely reveal a bell-curve result, predetermined by her choices.

She does not differentiate, nor does she see math as a conceptual discipline. She may end up teaching "math procedures" and doing it well, but her students will not develop the deep understanding *and* the passion that they could otherwise.

Finally, Miss Y appears to value student insights, their calculations, and their interactions—she may be a teacher who assesses processes, not just products. She does want them to personally grasp math theorems, but she also wants them to know what and why they're doing just that. Her use of bonus points for homework also suggests that she may end up with a skewed grading result, favoring higher "quarter grades" because the students have far more power over their own grades. They may well become competent, feel energized, and respond positively to her offers. In other words, they may motivate themselves because she has made that an attractive choice.

Certainly, Y has the least potential for developing alienated students of the three novice teachers in that building.

I urge us to "grade judiciously," to use marks to motivate thinking and entice ownership, to use marks drawn from various types of assessments, and to use marks to get teens to help each other grow. We don't know for sure, but it appears that Miss Y offers the best staring place for that type of *vision*.

Three Great Secondary Teachers: Voices of ENGAGING Classrooms

Imagine for a minute that you could watch three great veteran secondary teachers in a variety of locations: high school history in an urban setting, high school English in a suburban setting, and middle school science in a rural setting. Imagine that you could also interview the man and the two women about their practices, about their decisions, about their "intentions," about their ability to make every student *matter*, and to engage them all in a classroom setting. What would you look for? What would you ask them?

Here are the eight questions that I would ask if I could. I urge you to conduct your own inquires with teachers you have high regard for.

TEACHER INTERVIEW: ENGAGING Questions

Teacher _____ Date _____

Interviewer_____

1. How do you build productive relationships with every student? How do their individual (and group) differences affect these efforts? How do you help students build relationships with other students in the class community?

2. How do you allow students to develop their own individualized understanding of the important content you teach them?

3. Under what conditions would you use teams, peer interactions, cooperative learning, and/or paired tasks? How do you structure it?

4. How do you use active learning strategies? How do you embed authentic assessment into the instructional process?

5. How do you use graphic organizers and reading strategies? How do students record and/or document their ideas?

6. How do you use multiple intelligences and other differentiation strategies? How do you intervene to help students while they are doing their learning work?

7. Note making is one "writing-to-learn" strategy. What are some of the ones you use regularly? What do students *do* with the ideas they personally generate and record?

8. What are some of the factors that you consider in designing your grading system and determining individual grades? How does your plan affect student efforts to persist at their tasks, be careful and thoughtful, and take responsibility for their learning?

I have had the privilege to do just that: Dave Watkins, Beth Konkoski-Bates, and Maureen Russell are the superb teachers whom I have studied, talked with, and have seen work with the future teachers at Niagara University. I have interviewed them about how they treat teens and how they move students to take responsibility for their learning. They are terrific professionals who offer us much to think about. Here are their stories, interpreted through my filter of the ENGAGING factors.

David Watkins (History and Art, Weston Collegiate, Toronto, Ontario, Canada)

A tall, handsome, and athletic forty-five-year-old man, Dave Watkins is an exemplary secondary teacher in a great and diverse school (with a 150-year history) that sits in a busy section of metropolitan Toronto. Dave grew up in the Windsor-Detroit area, and his family has innumerable and deep roots throughout the region. An African-Canadian, his family knew success because they knew hard work and held great value for spiritual matters. Dave was personally touched by issues of racism, discrimination, and prejudice, and has dedicated his teaching and coaching career to the creation of thoughtful, responsible, and respectful young people, with a special eye to reaching members of the black community. His is a student-centered pedagogy, one of strong personal relationships, never ending love and care, persistence and perseverance—he seeks to touch every one of his students. To Dave, every student matters.

I have seen Dave teach numerous times and there are strong patterns to his efforts. Each of these aligns well with the ENGAGING process, and if one thing does stand out, it is the attentive engagement and investment that EVERY student makes in his class. He loves the large group discussion, with everyone pouring forth his or her ideas on controversial issues, where everyone is safe to take a "unique" stand, and where his own strong messages are intertwined with the realities of the young peoples' lives.

Here is a sample of Dave's actions that mark him as very special.

"Encouragement" is the operative word in his classroom community. He knows every student's individual "story"—he chats with them before class, in the hall, on the phone, on the bus (on a four-hour bus trip to Windsor he engaged dozens of students in stories, parables, harangues, and he listened as they shared themselves. This happened again three days later, when they returned). He holds high expectations for his students, and for the black youngsters he adds the "racial responsibility issue," suggesting that they do face an oppression that makes their success efforts harder and different than for other youth. (His approach epitomizes the Culturally Relevant Model proposed by Ladson-Billings [1995], engaging practice with an emphasis of issues of oppression.) He does this in a way that builds pride without divisiveness and which offers hope instead of frustration.

A great talker, Dave also is a great listener: He "hears" the kids and knows each of the learners well enough to ask the right question when appropriate. He motivates them through challenge, emotional provocation, patience, their interests and individuality, and by helping them set their own goals (both in school and after graduation). Ownership, the hallmark of the ENGAGING process, is the goal in his courses.

Dave's classes demand that students think for themselves and be able to defend their perspectives and suggestions. Interestingly, Dave's class is full of noise and loud verbal exchange, all of which is done in an emotionally safe manner: He is very quick to stop exchanges that deviate from a respectful community norm. His class also has the feel of a Baptist church, with people testifying, taking positions, pouring out their insights and truths, and yet never wavering very far from the essential question that is at the heart of each lesson. Students leave his class knowing that they are tired *and* charged up from thinking so much and from having to deal with issues and ideas that are new to them.

College teachers would call what Dave has students do "critical thinking," but it is a little more than that. He expects that the thinking also be personal and it must make sense for that individual, both today and for the future. My phrase "negotiating meaning" is precisely this process: Versions of historical events, verbal proclamations, understandings of current events, and plans for the future exist only in the minds of those who know them. Their meaning, although debated often, resides in each individual.

I often say, "Information is external; knowledge and understanding is internal." Dave knows that every message is only as good as it is interpreted and made personal, and he plans accordingly (Ontario Institute for Studies in Education).

An old friend, Professor John Myers of OISE, watched Dave teach and made several salient points: "First, Dave's lesson demonstrated the power of emotion and passion for connecting with the students. His pre-lesson 'banter' with many students was quite to the point. Secondly, the students had to think and contribute. Class was about dialoguing the needs and responsibilities of the community. The class was 'on' for the next hour. Everyone was intense (no one asked to leave for the washroom!), many offered ideas to the entire group and harsh (but true) things were said. It worked so well because of the personal connections he had with the students and the high level of trust" (Myers, 2006).

In short, Myers's comments stress the extremely high importance of that first E in "ENGAGING": encouragement from building relationships. Students will work hard, search for excellence, wrestle with difficult issues, extend themselves, and see meaning in their schoolwork under the conditions that Dave creates. The connections set the stage, allowing other, perhaps more technical aspects, to play a heavy role in creating student content understanding. Dave clearly realizes that without student intentionality and investment, there is no meaningful cognitive growth.

Dave sees himself as the leader of his students—he is their advocate, their conscience, their representation (model) of rewarded work, and their firmament. (He will never give up on any student. Ladson-Billings refers to this form of leadership as the "conductor," the highest form of effective teaching.) His instructional techniques vary within this setting—he uses much large group interaction, but does have students complete learner-centered projects.

In the classes that I have seen, he has used a class graphic organizer (the T-bar), he expects that students behave communally, he uses grades very judiciously (always allowing the student "the benefit of the doubt" and seems to always offer "another chance"), he never lets "note taking" become the modus operandi of a class, and he is appreciative and solicits the use of student artistic abilities. (He is an artist himself.)

Dave, along with colleague John Solarski, directs a field trip for fifty students (and numerous teachers) each spring: They travel 250 miles to participate in a complex, student-centered and challenging African Diaspora Conference in Windsor, Ontario. Getting students ready for the experience becomes the central thesis of his course and the reality of the session is used as the springboard for late spring classroom discussions. By traveling with the students and making school equal life, Dave overcomes what Newmann (1992) refers to as the negative indicators of alienation: fragmentation, estrangement, and separation. Dave's overall plan can be seen as a blueprint for making secondary school meaningful, personal, fulfilling, and thoughtful. Conference preparation helps students build trust with him and with the school as an entity. Again, Newmann is helpful: "If they [students and teachers] engage together in a range of activities such as recreation, dining, housekeeping,...trusting relationships are more likely to develop."

One way to help teens think they matter is by making them part of the teacher's life. The students know that Dave needs to care about them (Noddings, 1992), he needs them to succeed if he is to be a successful teacher, and they accept the fact that (Canadian) society in general needs them in order for it to be fully democratic, equitable, and excellent. There is nothing more motivational than being needed (Vermette, 1998) *and* students feel that they are needed by Dave. Moreover, the students fully believe that they are gaining a great deal by "doing school" with this teacher. Life is fun, too, when school and life become one and the teen knows that his or her role in that integration is central to its existence.

In October 2007, Dave was honored by Niagara University as its Canadian Teacher of the Year. In November 2007, he was selected as Canada's

Teacher of the Year, winning the Governor General's Award and traveling to the nation's capital to be recognized. He is amazing and ENGAGING and is successful because the teens *matter* greatly to him and he has the will to do whatever it takes to be helpful.

Beth Konkoski-Bates (English, Broad Run High School, Ashburn, Virginia)

A doting mother of two, forty-two-year-old Beth is in the fifth teaching position of her fifteen-year career. She has taught in private and public schools, at various grade levels from 1 to 12, in California, New York, Virginia, Maryland, and in middle class and high-poverty areas. As she and her husband have moved around the United States, she has developed a set of skills, an instructional bag of tricks, a clear and concise philosophy, and a commitment to adolescent thinking that have integrated her experiences and her knowledge into a complete package. In short, she is the finest secondary teacher that I have ever personally seen teach teens.

Over the past twelve years, I have chatted with her, observed her in action more than twenty times, created opportunities for my students (and other teachers) at Niagara to learn from her, and have written and studied with her. I won't try to be "unbiased" in this part of the text. I am going to describe how Beth stands up to the eight ENGAGING components and how she has influenced my thinking about teaching.

Beth clearly sets a high priority on relationship building across all students and their groups. She uses several strategies to accomplish this.

For one, much of class time is spent "working the room" (Konkoski-Bates & Vermette, 2004), moving around and consciously interacting with each student about his or her ideas, frustrations, successes, and next steps. She is one teacher (of many) who learn every name as soon as possible—human beings without names cannot be "complete." She uses name tags, identification nameplates, rosters, and index cards, and she publicly calls out the names as often as possible every day until she has them all down "cold." Moreover, their public speaking attempts, usually a nerve-wracking experience for a teenager, all come out of a communal feeling of enjoyment and investment—students offer their contributions (*not* the "right answer"!) to help others, to show off their good thinking, and to spark more thought.

Beth allows for thoughtful interpretation of all text handled in her course—every student has a point to make. But, true to her discipline, Beth demands that the contributions be consistent with the disciplinary point being made: She demands that *evidence* align properly. Moreover, she makes students "go back to the text" to justify and support ideas. Opinions don't matter as much as text-supported interpretations do. Student efforts to make these connections are highly valued, however.

In her class, all meaning is negotiated by students working alone and to-gether—critical thinking, creativity, and challenge are all supported, but no "sloppy scholarship" is tolerated. Her vision of a competent student is one who is reasoned, knowledgeable, and cares about reaching supportable be-liefs. It is anything but the "anything goes" philosophy attributed to constructivism by those who don't understand it. Beth's students search for meaningful truths, and do so in a rational and educated way.

Beth uses groupings in various ways. Occasionally, assigned teams do big projects, frequently small groups work on smaller tasks, and sometimes people choose to work together on assignments. She does occasionally "group grade," but always makes sure that no student is rewarded for (doing) nothing. She has strategies to assess each person's contribution and she chats with all the students about their work *and* their contributions to oth-ers. Moreover, her "speed-dating" technique is a valuable asset for those wishing to build community and create many opportunities for students to meet each other and get everyone's insights. It works like this:

1. Every student has a draft of a product ready to share (for exam-ple, an opening paragraph of an essay).

2. The table is arranged so that students face a partner *across* the table (envision twelve facing twelve *or* two groups of six facing six).

3. For a fixed amount of time (say, four minutes), students in row A show and chat with the partner across from them in row B about the product. Written comments are expected on the pa-per. (This is a form of peer editing.)

4. When time is called, students in row A say thanks and "slide down" to the next seat. Then they share and chat with their new partner and receive the written feedback.

5. When the first row is done, the second group (members of row B) get to have their work assisted.

This is a time-consuming process, but it is active, engaging, unique, pow-erful, and fun; moreover, because expectations are that people will be helpful to each other (and Beth "works the room" to make sure that happens), class feels like a community where everyone belongs. A hidden aspect of this tech-nique is that it raises individual accountability levels as well. To make this strategy work, *every* student matters: each student must have the product ready and be willing to help others. Work gets done, improvements get made, students feel like the class is their own (which, in fact, it is), and good ideas are sparked, appreciated, and shared.

As you can tell from the comments above, Beth's class is modeled after a "workshop" approach. Kids come in to do their work, get feedback (which is a superb form of ongoing active assessment), feel appreciated, and take ownership of their own successes. (And their failures, I might add—like the rest of us, Beth has real kids. Some don't do their work, some are unable to concentrate or finish, some have lost their appetite for actually doing something academic in nature. What is noteworthy is that these students are still valued for their humanity, their individuality, and their persona. Beth also is fully aware of each "individual story" and adjusts her interventions accordingly. [See Flynn, Mesibov, Vermette, & Smith (2004) for more on these interventions.] In the end, she does have some "failure to succeed" students, but they are few and far between and none are alienated *because* of her intervention.)

Again, Beth's eighty-minute classes are marked by some teacher direction, some large group dialogue, but every session is most heavily identified by "students doing think work" that is important, conceptual, personal, and valuable.

By the way, this approach, which aligns so well with knowledge-worker jobs in the workplace and with the thinking demands of a modern citizen in the flat-earth world of Friedman (2005), does fully prepare teens for the standardized tests they face (which will come as no surprise to those readers familiar with the work of Perkins [1999] and Knapp [1995]). Her kids pass the tests without the deadly drill-and-kill that permeates contemporary school culture (and which is a complete "turn-off" to so many adolescents).

Beth actually teaches other teachers about literacy strategies (including graphic organizers), so her use in every class should come as no shock. Working with a colleague, Sonia Basko, she has created at least four all-purpose organizers that are especially valuable for prereading and during-reading use. Her students develop deep understanding quickly because the scaffolds they use force them to categorize, connect, and defend their decisions on a regular basis (Perkins [1998] suggests that this is what *causes* their understanding).

Beth is a master of the use of multiple intelligences theory: Although reading and writing (verbal linguistic intelligence) are at the center of her discipline and her students' work, she utilizes all other components on a regular basis. Beth often assigns multiple tasks, gives great choice and uses a fluid rubric that allows a great deal of student input. Her students create songs, write and act out skits, contemplate their own thinking and feelings, visually represent ideas, share ideas and collaboratively plan a project, use evidence to build a logical case, and incorporate nature and/or classification schemes into their work. From my perspective that list includes musical, body–kinesthetic, intrapersonal, visual–spatial, interpersonal, logical–mathematical, and the natural intelligences. Gardner (1983) would be proud of Beth's uses of the intelligences as the exit format for culminating cognitive tasks.

Simply put, Beth has never "given notes" in the form that many teachers do. She does expect her students to keep records documenting their own thinking, whether they are called journal entries, outslips, drafts, or simply responses. She will ask a question during class and ask that students write their response; these are then used as springboards for discussion.

Because she sees student knowledge as continuously developing and improving, she sees these written efforts as "drafts" and treats them as "current" attempts at understanding. This approach empowers kids to take risks, trying out new ideas and allowing them to develop, even if they are later "replaced" by new (and better) ideas.

Finally, Beth does use grades to document student achievement and she has a huge range of scores. (There are failures, as stated above, and there are a significant number of As.) Two things stand out about her marking practice:

1. There are few, if any, surprises in the grading process. Students know what is expected, how they are doing, what they need to do next and what the implications of their current status are. In every place she has taught, students have been surprised at how much better their work gets *if* they make the changes that she recommends and if they thoughtfully commit themselves to improvement. (Note that it is not just that grades change, but that the work gets better.)

2. Beth uses rubrics that make sense to students. Students understand what is expected and they know that there is no "cookie cutter" culture at work in her room. Each project is unique, different, personal, and fairly marked.

In closing, I want to mention that I have spent many hours pouring through survey data that was collected from Beth's students as part of my inquiry. I refrained from using a Likert scale in favor of an open ended *outslip* format (like the ones that I have been advocating throughout the text) to allow the teens to really speak their minds. The data collected are fascinating and the general trends reveal several patterns that are worthy of our attention.

♦ The students know what it is like to be respected by the teacher and know they are important to her. Teens are appreciative of mattering to Beth and they also note that no disrespect is allowed towards each other in her class.

♦ With only a few exceptions, students think that she grades "fairly;" they know that they have to do their work, that they must strive for excellence, that their work is personalized and that she will be reasonable about their getting the work done.

♦ Class is perceived as "fun," time flies by, and "everyone" participates.

In many ways, this teacher exemplifies the ENGAGING process at its best.

Maureen Russell (Middle School Science, Naples, New York)

Maureen Russell is a veteran middle school science teacher and (and department chair) in the rural village of Naples, New York. A former outdoor educator, Maureen came to teaching in a somewhat convoluted way. She took an environmental ed course as a college senior and it made her begin thinking of combining her love of the environment with her commitment to biological progress. She did worry, at that time, about dealing with all those "kids." Today, as irony would have it, she is a fabulous example of the student-centered approach called constructivism and is most concerned with the emotional and social development of her students. Her classes are marked by student active engagement, their attempts at meaning making, respectful interaction, and healthy expectations for content learning. She sees the environment as the perfect content to help youngsters to develop themselves as thinking citizens and to behave as members of a community.

Let us briefly examine my interpretation of Maureen's responses to this small set of questions (which are loosely aligned with some of the eight ENGAGING factors).

◆ How does she build positive relationships with every student, so that the student will try to do good work?

Every student matters to Maureen and to the other students—they "leave their troubles" in a barrel by the door so that when they enter, they are free to be themselves and to work with others as equals. She strives to connect individual interests into mandated curriculum topics and tests and grades with individual strengths in mind. (She gives students many chances to show their excellence and they take great advantage of the opportunities being offered.)

◆ Science is full of "hypothesis testing." When her students make their own understandings, does she worry that they will be "accurate"? (*Note:* This is a *huge* fear of conservative critics of progressive education—they are sure students will learn "wrong truths" in learning-centered classrooms. Although this begs the question of what is the "right answer" to issues of history or literature, it also makes the practice of calling 65% "right" an acceptable, *passing* score a bit problematic. They tend to forget that many students have learned many "wrong truths" many times in many traditional classes.)

◆ Consistent with "negotiating meaning," Maureen does *not* emphasize the right answer, but pushes the notion of students offering a "best guess from what they know," and then follows up by having students check their ideas against the evidence that they gather or find. They develop the ability to think well and find out that it is OK to change their minds when evidence supports that change. Her persistent use of challenging questions fosters an attitude of inquiry and promotes respect for science as a continuous improvement discipline. As they progress though their year with her, students feel that they are in charge of their own learning and that science is made up of questions *and* answers *and* thoughts. They also realize that evidence matters and that learning is more process than product.

♦ I have seen her use groups on several occasions. What are her major concerns when she builds teams, plans tasks, and "works the room" while they do their think-work?

Psychological safety is the hallmark of this classroom so that is her first concern during groupwork or in paired projects. Everyone must be accepted and treated with dignity. Like Cindy Kline (see the next section on Cooperative Learning), Maureen wants the youngsters to develop socially and emotionally and her classroom is a laboratory for that learning. Moreover, Maureen makes sure that students keep records of their own planning so they can do reflections at a later date.

♦ Do her kids think that she is "fair" in her grading? What are some of the considerations when she sets up a grading system?

Grades matter to middle school kids: Low achievers want to succeed, and are desperately seeking acceptance; high achievers *need* good grades and define themselves accordingly. She thinks that teachers ought to take many things into consideration before offering a grade: personal circumstances, the amount of choice allowed within a graded item, reading abilities, reliance on print matter for learning, and past history are among those listed. Like O'Connor (2002), she wants to make sure that the grade is aligned with standards and that they are perceived as "fair." The students that I have talked to indicate that she is successful on this venture and that they really trust her judgment.

In closing this section, I'd like to add that Maureen's vision of the good teacher aligns very well with three characteristics mentioned earlier (intentional, thoughtful, and joyful). Her plans and materials are continuously revised for her specific students and classes; she patiently allows every student to speak his or her mind; and she grades her students respectfully and carefully. However, the joyfulness of her work stands out for special consideration.

There are three aspects of "fun" and "joy" that are worth noting. First, Maureen has become a "people person," meaning that her introverted nature *needs* the energy involved in the interaction and collaboration created by her teaching. She expects students to share their ideas, especially their related (personal) stories, so that her science class is always relevant, personal, and meaningful. Every class every day is different because different learners bring different "stories" to the fore. The students are expected to make the content connections—and they do.

Second, Maureen's room is open and hospitable—students are made to feel welcomed and are always treated with respect. Many choose to eat lunch in her room, talking with her or classmates, or sitting quietly reading. There are no threats allowed; it is a safe place to be. She encourages all students to try hard, to think for themselves, help each other, to ask questions, and to laugh a lot.

Third, it is clear to all that Mrs. Russell thinks that school and life should be enjoyed and that learning is fun. She uses many analogies, quotations, and references that are meant to make students smile. Moreover, she allows the energy and noise levels to rise substantially when the students work in groups, for they, too, get excited and enthusiastic about their ideas and their experiences. In her room, it is their education.

Cooperative Learning: Making Diversity a Strength

Much has been written about Cooperative Learning, including by me (e.g., Vermette, 1994, 1998). Without reiterating all that has been said about this instructional approach, I ask you to reread the brief section in Chapter 3, which deals with the "four fatal flaws," and then consider the following ten-item survey. Respond to these opinions/suggestions with agree or disagree (*not* true or false) and compare your answers to mine.

_____ 1. Students should pick their own teammates for Cooperative Learning work.

_____ 2. Students should concentrate on learning the materials, not getting the task finished.

_____ 3. With teens, Cooperative Learning is best used for outside projects.

_____ 4. Group grading is fair, easy, and teens like it.

_____ 5. Groupwork is the same thing as Cooperative Learning.

_____ 6. Cooperative Learning may be helpful for deep understanding but does not help kids remember key facts.

_____ 7. Middle school is developmentally inappropriate for Cooperative Learning; it is for high school only.

_____ 8. At the end of a class period, the teacher should close the class, not the bell.

_____ 9. Because Cooperative Learning makes the student thinking audible and visible, teachers should be ready to intervene as they "work the room."

_____ 10. Students will learn to like Cooperative Learning if it is used wisely and graded carefully.

Here are my responses in a nutshell: I agree with 8, 9, and 10 totally, I am unsure about 2, and I disagree with the others.

Sometimes teachers can let students choose to work alone or with friends, but because teens seldom go out of their comfort zones willfully, full preparation for life demands that they do some work with others that they wouldn't choose on their own. Almost always, this spread of interaction to new relationships strengthens the sense of community and builds a better infrastructure in the classroom. At Niagara University, we often tell students that "they don't have to like each other, just work with each other and show respect," to support the notion that interaction is a positive, that diversity is a strength and that such interdependent contact is a great harbinger of adult success. Clearly, sense of belonging is connected to this strategy and we must remember that seldom does a student do his or her best work in an emotionally or intellectually uncomfortable setting: community demands common respect for each member. The internal structure of groups must be diverse, and the teacher is responsible for structuring and building a positive atmosphere. (Obviously, teamwork should be the philosophical underpinning for the class.)

Teachers should take the time to "process out" the interactions of teammates and themselves as they work in class on an important task. Typically, I suggest that the teacher close the class by commenting on how students have fared in their collaborations that day. Formal assessments of self and peers (like the form offered by Cindy Kline in Figure 4.1) should also become a regular part of the class work. Kline, whose central focus is the development of powerful affective skills, spends great energy and attention on the implications of (a) students working in collaborative settings on a regular basis and (b) student ownership of his or her own learning and his or her own interactions. As a result, a student in her class is assessed by the teacher often, does self-assessment regularly, and frequently receives feedback secured (by Kline) from teammates. Kline spends much of her time helping young teens think about themselves, their actions and beliefs, and about others' feelings and perceptions. (See Armstrong [2006, chapter 5] for a full elaboration of this educational perspective for ten- to fourteen-year-olds. Moreover, virtually *all* of Alfie Kohn's fine writings are about helping teens develop concern for others, including other teens.)

Figure 4.1 Student-Team Evaluation Form

Scale: 1 = does not display; 2 = a little; 3 = occasionally; 4 = usually; 5 = always						
Names of the students in the group	My name					
Desirable Behaviors						
1. Encouraged others to offer ideas, give feedback, and participate						
2. Handled conflict in approved ways						
3. Was prepared and kept focused and on task						
4. Interacted with patience, tolerance, respect, and caring						
5. Made others feel like they belonged to the team						
6. Helped others have fun and/or enjoy the teamwork						
7. Provided contributions to the final form of the product						

Source: Kline and Vermette (2006).

This reflective component requires that students honestly assess themselves as people, as workers, as teammates, and as part of a community. Teachers, too, must keep students focused on how they are supposed to act in groups and how these dispositions and behaviors lead to adult success. Identifying and reinforcing specific qualities is part of the classroom management strategy in the ENGAGING classroom.

My "home base" district has five such qualities (or virtues) posted on every wall in the district:

♦ Kindness

♦ Humility

♦ Respect

♦ Responsibility

♦ Honesty

Students can use these five qualities to assess affective growth and to examine adult perspectives on how these operate in life. (They can also have meaningful discussions about what these words mean *and* what has been left out by this limited selection. For example, Goleman [1998, 2006] has a powerful list of twenty-five competencies that are currently at the center of a long-term investigation with middle school students [Jones, Jones, Vermette, & Kline, 2008; Kline & Vermette, 2006].)

Although most students enjoy and work well in cooperative groups, some resist, and do so for logical reasons. Students don't like to be taken advantage of by classmates nor do they want to be punished for other's lack of effort (Vermette, 1998). Also, they do want to have their positive contributions noted. All of these concerns can be dealt with in the well-structured Cooperative Learning classroom. "Processing out" and the limited use of group grading go a long way toward reducing the typical student dislikes of Cooperative Learning.

By the way, without "processing out" and/or instruction about social skills, and without some form of positive interdependence, Cooperative Learning becomes just "groupwork," which has been shown to be a less-effective teaching strategy than real Cooperative Learning. Often teachers put teens in small groups to do work that could be easily done by one person, with the result that one person does the work and the rest just copy answers. Well-structured Cooperative Learning means that everyone has to participate and each has to be responsible for some aspect of the total work.

Finally, I suggest that teachers start with easy, short, and clearly interesting in-class activities so that you can carefully observe their work, talk to the students about their interactions and see/hear what is actually happening.

Long-term and complex projects should come late in the process, not at the start.

I opened this section with ten items and appeared to be confused or uncertain about item 2; let's return to that one item. My position is that students should concentrate on gaining their own conceptual understanding by completing the assigned task *and* they should gain insight into their own actions as people. If so, they will learn a lot, stay ENGAGED, and begin to see how the richness of our diversity can make each of us better in many ways.

"Practice" in Two Paradigms

Take a few seconds and read these descriptions from ninth grader Tanika's day; think about her "practice" with content and her level of ENGAGEMENT in each class.

- In third period science, Tanika is labeling a blank, outlined diagram of the solar system, copying from her textbook. She uses different colors for various aspects of the system and is building a legend for the visual.

- In fifth period math, she is solving equations with one unknown by plugging numbers into the formula that the teacher has written on the board. If she gets all the items done in class, she will not have to do twenty items (just the "odd ones") on page 45 for homework.

- In sixth period English, she is writing a story about her favorite summer day and is concentrating on her use of adjectives and adverbs, including those new ones listed on the board. She wrote her first draft of the paper in class yesterday, and it was edited by a peer for grammar and punctuation. Today, she will make changes and assess it herself.

- In ninth period social studies, she is part of a group creating a skit about the French Revolution. They have to use various resources to help them make the play realistic and they are responsible for preparing the rubric for quality work.

See any differences? Each teacher might claim that she or he is using "active learning" or that the kids are "practicing" in the guided/independent practice schema of Madeline Hunter's (1982) model. However, practice in the first two examples is either mindless (although hands-on) copying or simple replication, whereas in the other examples careful, thoughtful, personalized, somewhat unpredictable, and meaningful cognitive work is happening. Thus I offer two conceptually different meanings for the term "practice," one for each paradigm.

In paradigm one, the traditional/behaviorist paradigm, practice is a form of replication, recitation, and/or rehearsal. In paradigm two, the ENGAGING/constructivist paradigm, practice is a form of investigation, analysis, or integrative synthesis. The levels of deep thinking and the resulting meaningful and personalized understanding are incomparable across these two conditions: it happens regularly and intentionally under the conditions that exist in paradigm two (and it could happen by accident in the other).

Thus, I suggest that you be wary of people speaking of "active learning," if they also say things like "hands-on" instead of "minds-on." Student *understanding* results from deep engagement in problem solving, product creation, or decision making (with evidence), and it requires the types of "practice" that force those (cognitive) actions. Rote rehearsal has little place in modern schools.

These are huge differences that are not to be underplayed. "Practice doesn't make perfect." In fact, it doesn't do anything valuable unless it is carefully structured and thoughtfully meaningful to the learner (like ENGAGING practice is supposed to do).

The ENGAGING process is really the ENGAGING paradigm, but if I called it that you might have been turned off by the wording and not be reading the book right now. A paradigm shift, a comprehensive change of perspective, can be a scary thing, but it is what is happening in our profession right now. The jump toward learning-centered classrooms is momentous, innovative, and permanent. Practice, as we once thought of it, may be a thing of the past, replaced by "learning experiences" that remind us that all teens matter (see Wasserman [2007] for an analysis of a potentially powerful learning experience that was not carefully structured and resulted in little real gain by learners).

One Period in the Reallygoods' Day: Using the ENGAGING Paradigm to Differentiate Middle School Instruction

In this hypothetical scenario, we get to see a pair of teachers coteaching a middle-level group of students. As you will see, they are student-centered, committed to the project approach, have adapted a variety of modern strategies (including a version of integrated curriculum) and are fully aware of ENGAGING. As you read, try to (a) identify the structure of their learning experience, (b) identify applications of ENGAGING, and (c) evaluate their attempts at "differentiation," the contemporary concept that needs close examination. The Reallygoods seem very much aware that each student is unique and to be valued, that each becomes a better person when she or he gets to work with others, and that school is about thinking and making meaning of important ideas.

Background

Drs. Chris and Lee Reallygood, a married couple, have been team-teaching at the Jesse Owens Middle School for the past 15 years. Technically, Chris is the social studies teacher and Lee is the English/language arts teacher. They have team taught at both the seventh and eighth grade levels, and have developed a multidisciplinary approach that serves both disciplines, and they have made a conscious effort to integrate with the science and math programs. They are good friends with the teachers from those disciplines and have worked very closely with them. The past summer they all participated in a powerful week-long conference hosted by the Institute for Learning-Centered Education where they created new materials and some new, student-centered units.

The Reallygoods have been successful with the diverse set of students that come from every socioeconomic level of the small city, Miller, in which they work (and live). They think that "differentiation" is the key to their successes, because it allows them to recognize each student as a unique individual, allows them to offer a choice of projects to show understanding, it aligns beautifully with Understanding by Design's Six facets of Understanding *and* the eight parts of multiple intelligences theory, and *does not* require them to teach at the lower levels of Bloom. (They think nothing is more boring to middle schoolers than memorizing for a test, and nothing sillier than letting them then forget everything immediately.) They used to like Hunter's Anticipatory Set, but felt that it did not touch enough students very effectively, so for years they have been planning much longer openings, involving differentiated activities to involve everyone. (They then read Flynn et al. [2004] and found out that they were using the concept of the Exploratory Phase.)

RINNGGGG!!!!!! As the bell finishes ringing to call open this eighty-minute class, the twenty-six students are still scrambling around the room: there was much energy and no real pattern of behavior until Chris announced, "Everyone to his or her seat. We're going to have a formal start today."

Twenty-three seconds later, the room was still, except for a small amount of fidgeting. "Number your paper one to ten. Put your name on it. We're going to collect it and count it toward half of today's daily grade. Ready?"

The question was greeted with some furtive pleas for patience but within seconds, everyone was ready. Lee continued, "In spaces one, two, and three write down three places in life where triangles exist. GO." After a forty-second pause, she tells them that they have another minute to check with fellow students and to expand the list to ten.

"OK, stop. Now look around the room—as some of you started to do, Christian, Marli—and find the triangles here. Make a list of twenty. Then grab your partner and get the protractors and measure the side lengths and the angles. Create some drawings to show your measurements. You have about twelve minutes. Get going."

Partners found each other and the equipment, and began walking around the room purposefully. The Reallygoods trailed several, including a hulky and ragged brute name Monk, but then split up and worked the entire room at a very quick pace. They stopped at every pairing (some more than once) and checked the progress of their documentation.

Some students were having difficulty converting their findings onto the data collection sheet and the teachers gave a few hints.

Within a short time, the students began talking about their findings. Carl Smythe, the class brain, had announced that all of them will have angles totaling 180 degrees, but then Chris asked the whole class, "Is that true for inside angles and outside angles?" He also announced that he would not accept shout-out answers. "Get the data," he said. Also, he asked several groups to put their numbers on the overhead so that everyone else could see what they had found.

Suddenly, Lee asked the class to individually write or draw a symbolic picture of the process that they just had been doing. She had them do it on their turn-in sheet and gave them about three minutes. "You can go back and finish later, but right now, share with your partner."

Chris interrupted this process by saying: "What does math—these angles—have to do with social?" No one knew (there were no hands up). "Well, I want you to do one of two things: either get the text, chapter 23, or go to the computer and find eighteenth century U.S. architecture. Whichever one you choose, look at the visuals you find and see if you can come up with a theory about how those folks used math when they made buildings."

As the students began their checking, several questions came up:

- "Which folks do we study? Northerners or southerners? Free or slave?"

- "How do I find anything? What am I doing?"

- "I thought architecture was about, like, science stuff or art?"

- "What do I do with my theory?"

In each case, Lee nodded and said, "Make a good decision, talk to your partner, and you'll tell us all about the process later."

There seemed to be some angst and confusion in the room, but the students helped each other, the teachers redirected student comments very well, and pretty soon some ideas began to flow. A student (Carl) suggested that the comments be written down on the front board and they were.

After this piece of the lesson seemed to quiet down, Chris spoke. "Take a look at everything we found. Could you write five questions about eighteenth century architecture? Questions that also connect to modern-day architecture here in town?"

Four minutes later, Lee placed a sheet of her own questions on the overhead:

♦ Why did people build buildings the way they did?

♦ How are modern buildings the same or different to the ones we found back then?

♦ Given all that happened in history, where does architecture fit in?

♦ In the houses you've found, how do you think the people were like or not like us?

♦ What did you find interesting so far in our work? What made you think a lot? What do you still wonder about?

After she read them, she began calling on students to raise the number of statements/questions to an astonishing fifteen.

Chris chimed in. "OK. Before we go and research the answers to a total of ten of these items, you and your partner have to decide what form your 'demonstration of understanding' will take. You have three choices, and we will work on this tomorrow and be almost done by the end of tomorrow's class. As usual, if you do a "good enough" job, you both get seventy points and then we negotiate with you individually if you want to try for more points, up to a max of 100. Plus, of course, you get your class daily grade and homework bonuses."

"The choices, posted now on a board on the *info wall*, include (a) a booklet that illustrates a comparison of architecture from different time periods with explanations of how math helped them build these constructions, (b) a song—music and lyrics—about answers to the questions, and (c) the creation of two actual models that demonstrate what you've found about buildings, history, and math. Of course, we will videotape your eight-minute presentation so that we can show it to our guests on visitor night next month. Any questions?"

As usual, there were too many questions, but almost all of them could not be answered until the students began to do their work. (After the students got started, they almost always became very clear on issues of how much? when? what form? and the Reallygoods knew well enough to let them endure the discomfort of uncertainty. From the Flynn book, the Reallygoods also understood that this was supposed to happen in the Discovery Phase. Moreover, they could create a powerful rubric *with* the students as they entered the next work period.)

The students began working in pairs, although some students approached Chris for help on the math aspects of the task. He called over two fellow students (and their partners) and asked them if they would be willing to help, if and when they were needed to explain some math stuff to classmates. There was no problem with that request.

With two minutes to go, Lee called them to order. "Please stop. Get the paper that you're going to turn in and either draw or write about what you thought deeply about today, both the content we came across *and* the questions you tried to answer. You may chat but please hurry; we want to read these tonight before we meet again." The students talked, wrote, or draw and dropped off the sheets at the door as they left for their reading class.

Authors' Comments

The project approach, in which numerous tasks are combined to allow students a chance to do real inquiry and to produce real samples of their understandings, is a perfect vehicle to differentiate instruction. Using the Two-Step (Flynn et al., 2004), as the Reallygoods do in this example, differentiates naturally. Use of the ENGAGING factors encourages students to do individual meaning making, fosters their need to make and record ideas, utilizes collaboration, and is totally active. Their plan supports choice theory, takes advantage of multiple intelligences and also builds community within the classroom.

The final point for us to focus on is how much ownership the students are taking in this classroom. By structuring the learning experience carefully, students slowly accept, modify, and then *own* their own investigations. This pair of educators help the students as they move through the stages and components, and will eventually have to assess their project, but there is no question that the work belongs to each student as an individual (and as an integral part of a team). Grading wisely is easy in this case, for students accept their projects, recognize the purpose of expectations, and have total control over the final mark.

At its core, "differentiation" means that students' needs are being met by their taking personal responsibility for their own individual educations, as is happening here. Everything about the eight ENGAGING factors entices differentiated applications and personalized meanings and develops a sense of efficacy for each teen.

Six Facets of Understanding

Wiggins and McTighe (2005) have made a mark in the educational literature by writing about "backwards planning" and "Understanding by Design." I praised Tomlinson and McTighe's 2006 book, which extended this vision to differentiating instruction, and reviewed it in Chapter 3. The heart of all of their efforts (with Tomlinson) is the notion that meaningful student understanding (not simple recall)—the Holy Grail of schooling—is six things, not one.

Yes, six: There are six facets of understanding. There are six valid "indicators" that allow students to demonstrate their understanding of essential content. Recall Howard Gardner? He says that there are "eight [distinct] ways to be smart," and offers the eight intelligences. Yes, differentiation and meeting the needs of all learners, can be productively conceptualized through an integration of these two theories.

The Six Facets of Understanding can be catalogued this way: explanation, interpretation, application, empathy, perspective, and self [-reflective] assessment. What this means for teachers is simple: For any *big idea* you teach, the more ways a student can show his or her understanding, the better…*and*…*and*…*and*…each of the six ways is a valid indicator and reflects students' strengths, and, possibly, student choice.

Let's apply this to a favorite poem of mine, written by Dudley Randall:

Booker T. and W.E.B.

"It seems to me" said Booker T.,
"It shows a mighty lot of cheek
To study Chemistry and Greek
When Mister Charlie needs a hand
To hoe the cotton on his land
And when Miss Ann looks for a cook,
Why stick your nose inside a book?"
"I don't agree," said W.E.B.
"If I should have the drive to seek
Knowledge of chemistry or Greek,
I'll do it. Charles and Miss can look
Another place for hand or cook,
Some men rejoice in skill of hand,
And some in cultivating land,
But there are others who maintain
The right to cultivate the brain."
"It seems to me," said Booker T.,

"That all you folks have missed the boat
Who shout about the right to vote,
And spend vain days and sleepless nights
In uproar over civil rights.
Just keep your mouths shut. Do not grouse,
But work, and save, and buy a house."
"I don't agree," said W.E.B.
"For what can property avail
If dignity and justice fail?
Unless you help to make the laws,
They'll steal your house with trumped-up clause.
A rope's as tight, a fire as hot,
No matter how much cash you've got.
Speak soft, and try your little plan,
But as for me, I'll be a man."
"It seems to me," said Booker T.
"I don't agree,"
said W.E.B.

Here is a set of questions, reflecting the six facets as they could be used to determine the understanding that students are developing:

- Can a student explain the poem's central point, as he or she sees it? (explanation)

- Can a student tell a story about this poem or link it to an analogy? (interpretation)

- Can the student connect this poem to today's African-American world? (application)

- Can the student describe how people who disliked the poem, and/or who favored one of the characters over the other, felt about the poem? (empathy)

- Can the student connect this poem to overall issues of black identity in U.S. history? (perspective)

- Can the student tell about the process by which he or she thought about the poem and make a current meaning for it? (metacognitive self-reflection)

Once again, the authors stress that there are six different and valid ways to show understanding, but one doesn't have to do all six (especially as a requirement for an A).

Educators are just beginning to play with these ideas and at this point in time, aligning it with Gardner's eight intelligences is just speculation, albeit, a hopeful speculation. (Figure 4.2 offers a 6×8 matrix that helps us see the structure of these possibilities at a glance.)

Figure 4.2 The Interaction of the Six Facets with the Eight Intelligences

	Verbal Linguistic	Logical Mathematical	Bodily Kinesthetic	Musical Rhythmic	Visual Spatial	Intrapersonal	Interpersonal	Naturalistic
Explain								
Interpret								
Apply								
Perspective								
Empathy								
Self-Knowledge								

Source: Vermette and Kline, 2008

Speculation aside, the notion of deriving a host of options, all valid, for students to authentically demonstrate their learning, has great potential for increasing motivation and ENGAGEMENT, and for making all kids realize how much they matter.

Let me offer three plausible variations drawn from the above discussion.

Faced with the choice as to how she'll represent her thinking, our ninth grade friend Tanika (from an earlier part of this chapter) does the following:

♦ She develops a creation story for the solar system, and details it with three-dimensional visuals that she builds (interpretation and visual spatial, with a touch of homage paid to her Native American cultural heritage).

♦ She interviews three classmates about their efforts at math work and writes a song about how it feels to try to learn some new math processes (empathy and musical, with homage to her background as a singer).

◆ She writes a 300-word passage for an encyclopedia about how the French Revolution fits into human freedom history after the skit is performed. (There is lot going on in this activity: explanation and verbal linguistic for sure, but the writing and acting [bodily/kinesthetic] in the skit and the teamwork [interpersonal] take this to a new plane.)

I have taken many liberties throughout this text, but I ask you a few simple questions based on this example:

◆ Would Tanika be *more* motivated, *more* engaged, and feel *more* powerful ownership if she were in a traditional classroom situation?

◆ Would Tanika develop better and deeper understandings of the content if she were studying it for a test in the typical manner?

◆ Would Tanika's classmates be *more* likely to be responsible for their actions, more unified as a community, or develop better social skills if they were following a traditional teacher-centered structure?

◆ Would Tanika feel *more* important in a traditional classroom?

Obviously, I am biased and want you to cry out loudly with the answer I prefer (which is, of course, NO!). But I do want you to contrast the possibilities offered by the ENGAGING process with the traditional classroom concept *and* consider the possibility of increased rigidity spawned by the so-called accountability movement and *No Child Left Behind*. Seriously folks, it is time to become fully learning-centered, utilize the eight ENGAGING factors, and design classrooms in which teens do their important and differentiated work. We should ignore test scores unless we are confident that they are (a) fair (they aren't), (b) measure student learning of important content (are you sure?), and (c) are used for diagnosis and future help (instead of stratification and embarrassment). We should look for (and create) new measures of understanding that matter to the world. And we should listen deeply to students talk about their thinking, their goals, and their hopes—and respect their existing talents.

I can think of eight things that you could do tomorrow to get this process going…

Final Examination

In the spirit of Tomlinson and McTighe (2006), I ask you to assess yourself on your understanding of the ENGAGING process as you now comprehend it. Please answer these questions…or at least choose to do some of them. Note that to do these well, you will need an associate, preferably a professional friend.

1. Please find an educator friend and explain the eight aspects of ENGAGING to him or her.

2. Create an analogy for each of the eight factors *and/or* tell a story about how you thought about them in your own work as you read this text.

3. Find out how your educator friend (in 1 above) uses each of the eight factors in his/her work.

4. Think about (or chat with) teachers who have difficulty shifting to a student-centered approach with teenagers. What do they see and think that is different from the author and what do they fear about constructivist practices? What is it about schooling that makes them reject a shift toward letting students take over their own educations?

5. There is always talk of pendulum shifts in education; this is done mostly to allow people an excuse to *not* change. But where does this ENGAGING thing fit into your sense of schooling's developing story? Will it be gone soon? Will it soon be the norm? Will a new "back-to-the-basics" movement return and drive more teachers toward "drill-and-kill" classwork and drive teens away from schooling? What is the future of the ENGAGING process?

6. What went through your mind during various parts of the text? (*Note:* If you actually recorded your responses to some of the questions and tasks, then you can use the written documents to help spark your memory of your thinking. This is "note making" in practice.) Did some tasks or comments strike you as too simple? Were some very profound? Were some too theoretical or impractical? Where was it impossible to make sense of or envision in a real classroom? Did you recognize yourself in the examples? How did you daydream about your use of the strategies? How did you decide on which strategies to experiment or play with in your classes?

As there are Six Facets of Understanding, the previous six questions can spark different and valid insights into how well you understand ENGAGING. Assess yourself…enjoy…and try to:

E **entice** all teens to engage with each other and with important ideas

N **negotiate** their own meaning of content

G **group** for collaboration and community so learners can share & dialogue before, during and after "instruction"

A **activate** learning and activate **authentic assessment**

G (use) **graphic organizers** to help students scaffold thinking and document understanding

I **intervene** with **intelligences** to meet diverse learners' needs and to make their work relevant

N (use) student **note making** to build a personal record of his or her learning process

G **grade wisely** to recognize achievements (not failings) and to spur a continuous improvement mentality within the community

If you do these things, you'll be treating teens—their minds *and* their hearts—as if they *matter*.

References

Armstrong, T. (2002). *Multiple intelligences in the classroom.* Alexandria, VA: ASCD.

Armstrong, T. (2006). *The best schools: How human development research should inform practice.* Alexandria, VA: ASCD.

Bain, K. (2004). *What the best college teachers do.* Cambridge, MA: Harvard University Press.

Bargh, J.A., and Schul, Y. (1980). On the cognitive benefits of teaching. *Journal of Educational Psychology.* 72(5), 593–604.

Basko, S., and Konkoski-Bates, G. (2005). Four strategies to increase reading for understanding in secondary classrooms. Presentation at Niagara University, March 18.

Battistich, V., Solomon, D., Kim, D., Watson, M., & Schaps, E. (1995). Schools as communities, poverty levels of student populations, and students' attitudes, motives, and performance: A multilevel analysis. *American Educational Research Journal, 32,* 627–658.

Benware, C.A., and Deci, E.L. (1984). Quality of learning with active versus passive motivational set. *American Educational Research Journal, 21*(4), 755–765.

Bransford, J., Brown, A., and Cocking, R. (2000). *How people learn: Brain, mind, experience, and school.* Washington, DC: National Academy Press.

Brooks, J., & Brooks, M. (1993). *The case for the constructivist classroom.* Alexandria, VA: ASCD.

Bruner, J. (1996). *The culture of education.* Cambridge, Mass: Harvard University Press.

Carter, K. (1995). Teaching stories and local understandings. *Journal of Educational Research, 88,* 326–330.

Cohen, E. (1994). *Designing groupwork: Strategies for heterogeneous classrooms.* New York: Teachers College Press.

Covey, S. (1999). *Seven habits of highly effective people.* London: Simon & Schuster.

Danforth, S., and Smith, J. (2005). *Engaging troubling students: A constructivist approach.* Thousand Oaks, CA: Corwin Press.

Darling-Hammond, L. (1999, January). Educating teachers. *Academe, 85,* 1, 26.

Darling-Hammond, L., and Bransford, J., eds. (2005). *Preparing teachers for a changing world: What teachers should learn and be able to do.* San Francisco: Josey-Bass.

Darling-Hammond, L., and Ifill-Lynch, O. (2006). If they'd only do their work! *Educational Leadership,* 8–13.

Delpit, L. (1995). *Other people's children: Cultural conflict in the classroom.* New York: New Press.

Dewey, J. (1916). *Education and democracy.* Boston: Heath.

Dewey, J. (1938). *Experience and education.* New York: Collier Books.

Elias, M.J., and Arnold, H., eds. (2006). *The educators' guide to emotional intelligence and academic achievement: Socio-emotional learning in the classroom.* Thousand Oaks, CA: Corwin.

Flynn, P., Mesibov, D., Vermette, P., and Smith, R.M. (2004). *Applying standards-based constructivism: A two-step guide for motivating middle and high school students.* Larchmont, NY: Eye On Education.

Fredericks, J.A., Blumenfeld, P.C., and Paris, A. (2004). School engagement: Potential of the concept, state of the evidence. *Review of Educational Research, 74*(1), 59–109.

Friedman, T.L. (2005). *The world is flat: A brief history of the twenty-first century.* New York: Farrar, Strauss, & Giroux.

Gardner, H. (1983). *Multiple intelligences: The theory in practice.* New York: Basic Books.

Gardner, H. (2006). *Multiple intelligences: New horizons.* New York: Basic Books.

Glasser, W. (1986). *Control theory in the classroom.* New York: Harper and Row.

Goleman, D. (1998). *Working with emotional intelligence.* New York: Bantam Books

Goleman, D. (2006). *Social intelligence.* New York: Bantam Books.

Good, T.L., and Brophy, J. (2008). *Looking in classrooms, 10th ed.* Boston: Allyn & Bacon.

Goodlad, J.I. (1984). *A place called school: Prospects for the future.* New York: McGraw-Hill.

Hunter, M. (1982). *Instructional theory into practice.* El Sequendo, Ca: T.I.P. Press.

Jackson, P. (1994). *Life in classrooms.* New York: Holt, Rinehart and Winston.

Johnson, D., and Johnson, R. (1999). *Learning together and alone: Cooperative, competitive, and individualistic learning, 5th ed.* Boston: Allyn & Bacon.

Jones, K., Jones, J., Vermette, P., and Kline, C. (2008). *Building a case for social-emotional learning in the middle school mathematics classroom.* Manuscript under review.

Kagan, S. (1992). *Cooperative leaning for teachers.* Riverside, CA: University of California.

Kierwa, K. (1987). Note-taking and review: The research and its implications. *Instructional Science, 16,* 233–249.

Kline, C.L., and Vermette, P. (2006, October 20). *Using SEL and the ENGAGING process to improve middle school learning...and raise tests scores.* Presented at the New York State Middle School Association conference, Niagara Falls, NY.

Knapp, M. (1995). *Teaching for meaning in high poverty classrooms,* New York: Teachers College Press.

Kobayashi, Y. (1994). Conceptual acquisition through social interactions. *Human Development, 37,* 233–241.

Kohn, A. (2006, Fall). The tougher standards fad hits home: Invoking "accountability" and "competitiveness" to justify homework. *Rethinking Schools,* 32–39.

Konkoski-Bates, B., and Vermette, P. (2004, May 24). *Working the room.* Presentation at the Great Lakes Association for Cooperative Learning conference, Toronto, Ontario.

Kozol, J. (2005). *The shame of the nation: The restoration of apartheid schooling in America.* New York: Three Rivers Press.

Ladson-Billings, G. (1994). *Dreamkeepers: Successful teachers of African-American children.* San Francisco: Jossey-Bass.

Ladson-Billings, G. (1995). But that's just good teaching! The case for culturally relevant pedagogy. *Theory Into Practice, 34*(3), 159–165.

Mayer, R. (2004). Should there be a three-strike rule against pure discovery learning? The case for guided methods of instruction. *American Psychologist, 59*(1), 14–20.

McNeil, L. (1986). *Contradictions of control: School structure and school knowledge,* New York and London: Routledge.

Meier, D. (1995). *The power of their ideas: Lessons for America from a small school in Harlem,* Boston: Beacon Press.

Mesibov, D. (2003). Personal Communication, January 14.

Mitchell, S.N., Reilly, R., Bramwell, F., Lilly, F., and Solnosky, A (2004). Friendship and choosing groupmates: Preferences for teacher-selected vs. student-selected groupings in high school science classes. *Journal of Instructional Psychology, 31*,1, 17–29.

Myers, J. (2006, May 15). Personal communication.

Newmann, F., ed. (1992). *Student engagement and achievement in American secondary schools.* New York: Teachers College Press.

Noddings, N. (1992). *The challenge to care.* San Francisco: Jossey-Bass.

O'Connor, K. (2002). *How to grade for learning: Linking grades to standards.* Glenview, IL: Lesson Lab.

Ogle, D. (1986). K-W-L: A teaching model that develops active reading of expository text. *Reading Teacher, 39,* 564–570.

Osterman, K. (2000). Students' need for belonging in the school community. *Review of Educational Research, 70*(3), 323–367.

Perkins, D. (1998). *What is understanding?,* in Wiske, M.S., ed. (Ch 2), *Teaching for understanding: Linking research and practice.* San Francisco: Jossey-Bass.

Perkins, D. (1999). The many faces of constructivism. *Educational Leadership, 57*(3), 6–11.

Piaget, J. (1963). *Origins of intelligence in children,* New York: Norton.

Pink, D. (2005). *A whole new mind: Moving from the information age to the conceptual age,* New York: Riverhead Books.

Rothstein, R. (2004). *Class and schooling: Using social, economic and educational reform to close the black–white achievement gap.* Washington, DC: Economic Policy Institute.

Schaps, E., and Lewis, C. (1999). Perils on an essential journey: Building school community. *Phi Delta Kappan,* 215–218.

Scherer, M. (2002). Do students care about learning? A conversation with Mihaly Csikszentmihalyi. *Educational Leadership,* 12–17.

Schwartz, D.L., and Bransford, J. (1998). A time for telling. *Cognition and Instruction, 16*(4), 475–522.

Shapiro, A.M. (2004). How including prior knowledge as a subject variable may change outcomes of learning research. *American Educational Research Journal, 41*,1, 159–189.

Shenkar, O. (2004). *The Chinese century: The rising Chinese economy and its impact on the global economy, the balance of power and your job.* Boston: Wharton School Publishing.

Shuell, T. (2003). Toward an integrated theory of learning, presentation at *Northeastern Educational Research Association annual meeting,* Ellenville, NY (October 23).

Siegel, C. (2005). Implementing a research-based model of cooperative learning. *The Journal of Educational Research, 98* (6), 339–350.

Spires, H.A., and Donley, J. (1998). Prior knowledge activation: Inducing engagement with informational texts. *Journal of Educational Psychology, 90*(2), 249–260.

Stodolosky, S. (1998). *The subject matters:Classroom activity an math and social studies.* Chicago: University of Chicago Press.

Stodolosky, S.S., and Grossman, P.L. (2000). Changing students, changing teaching. *Teachers College Record, 102*(1), 125–172.

Thornburgh, N. (2006, April 17). Dropout nation. *Time Magazine,* 30–40.

Tomlinson, C.A., and Kalbfleisch, M.L. (1988). Teach me, teach my brain: A call for differentiated classrooms. *Educational Leadership,* 51–55.

Tomlinson, C.A., and McTighe, J. (2006). *Integrating differentiated instruction + understanding by design.* Alexandria, VA: ASCD.

Vermette, P. (1994). Four fatal flaws: Avoiding the common mistakes of novice users of cooperative learning. *The High School Journal,* 255–260.

Vermette, P.J. (1998). *Making cooperative learning work: Student teams in K–12 classrooms.* Upper Saddle River, NJ: Prentice-Hall/Merrill.

Vermette, P., & Kline, C. (2008). *Differentiating instruction through ENGAGING practice and SEL,* workshop at Corning-NYSMSA Institute, June 30–July 1.

Vygotsky, L. (1962). *Thought and language.* Cambridge, MA: MIT Press.

Wasserman, S. (2007). Let's have a famine! Connecting means and ends in teaching big ideas. *Phi Delta Kappan, 89*(4), 290–297.

Werner, T. (2005). Personal Communication, October 3.

Wiggins, G. & McTighe, J. (2005). *Understanding by design, 2nd Ed.* Alexandria: VA: ASCD.

Willingham, D.T. (2006). The usefulness of BRIEF instruction in reading comprehension strategies. *American Educator, AFT,* 30–45, 50.

Wolk, S. (2003). Hearts and minds. *Educational Leadership,* 14–18.

Woloshyn, V.E., Pavio, A., and Pressley, M. (1994). The use of elaborative interrogation to help students acquire information consistent with prior knowledge and information inconsistent with prior knowledge. *Journal of Educational Psychology, 86,* 79–89.